RAZZ MA TAZZ

My Life in Music, Television and Film

STAN ZABKA

Big Island Music, Inc.
www.zabka.com

ISBN: 978-0-615-68640-0

First Edition
18 17 16 15 14 13 10 9 8 7 6 5 4 3 2 1

Cover design and photo assembly by Billy Zabka
Interior design and layout by Dovetail Publishing Services

A Dedication

ZABKA BROTHERS IN WORLD WAR II

Frank, Al, John, Bob, Stan, George, Clifford, Clifton

. . . to those at home and abroad preserving our country's freedoms

. . . to the poets and musicians singing its praises

. . . to the film and television people telling their stories

. . . to the broadcasters keeping us informed

. . . to the American Forces Network for providing the home connection

There are two types of people you meet along life's track,
Those who take all your strength from you,
And those who put it all back.

—Anon

CONTENTS

ACKNOWLEDGMENTS

In April of 2006 I completed my autobiography, *A Long Line of Glory*. Believing it would make a good movie, I wrote an accompanying screenplay. When I was unable to interest a book publisher I shelved the entire project. Seven years later and a tad bit wiser, after investigating the upstart, fast-growing self-publishing business, *Razz Ma Tazz* is the result. In writing this memoir I learned two things: I could either assemble all the parts myself (editors, formatters, scribes, indexers, etc.), or I could work with a second tier publisher and pay for corresponding experts. I ended up being my own contractor, a time-consuming, laborious task, especially as I was only semi-conversant with computers.

My manuscript went through various stages of editing: family, friends, and scholars. More than once I felt my book was completed. After the third rewrite I hired a professional book editor, Michael Garrett, who offered excellent advice on what is acceptable to a publisher and what is not. I then sent the manuscript to my son Guy to determine whether my observations on the music industry were accurate in today's culture. My wife Nancy line-edited the manuscript page by page, which resulted in more changes. She completed this exercise more than once. It was a task that involved a great deal of concentration, especially as regards time-line events. My son Billy created the cover design and assembled the images, and Joan Keyes of Dovetail Publishing Services designed the interior.

I thought I had touched all the bases until I entered the marketing phase of publishing. Fortunately, I found Sharon Goldinger, an outstanding "book shepherd" who advised me to delay publication until I had more clearly defined my target audience. Realizing I faced a complete re-write, I heeded her advice. The choice was not difficult. As music was the center of my life, I made it the theme of my book. Sharon then introduced me to Jennifer Silva Redmond who guided me through a “memoir” vs “autobiography” phase. I chose the former, and some time later the book was completed, or so I thought.

Needing to know if my story was on the mark I gave the project to The York Consulting Team, Deborah Jude-York, Bob York and Rachael Howard for review. Besides substantive editing they assisted me in expanding certain sections and in juxtaposing (or totally eliminating) others. Their sage input contributed to my knowledge of composition, and in making *Razz Ma Tazz* a more compelling book.

Now came the fine tuning. It is that phase of composition which I enjoy most. In music it is akin to determining whether an orchestration needs an additional horn or violin, or simply to leave it alone. From the professional worlds of broadcasting, journalism, television, music and film, Nick Clooney, Hal Gurnee, Tom Foty and Bob Daley have added personal observations in praise of *Razz Ma Tazz*.

To one and all, thank you. I am eternally grateful.

FOREWORD

ON TO THE OSCARS

My family
Guy, Billy, Joey, Nancy and me, Judy, Holly

To have known the best, and to know it for the best, is success in life.
—John W. MacKay

Anyone setting out to write about his life does so to set the record straight, to tell a story, or both. To attract the largest audience, being a celebrity, or at least someone instantly recognizable, is almost mandatory. Neither a celebrity nor someone famous, in a career twice interrupted by military service I have had the extraordinary and unique opportunities to work with some of America's most noted talent in music, broadcasting, television and film. Among them were two with whom special bonds of trust and friendship emerged, "The Songbird of the South," Kate Smith, who recorded my first published song, and legendary Johnny Carson, on whose *Tonight Show* I was Associate Director and occasional guest.

One of the reasons Johnny and I became good friends was because I knew him at the beginning, before his meteoric rise to fame. Johnny is quoted as having offered the following advice to all who would listen: "Talent alone won't make you a success. Neither will being in the right place at the right time, unless you are ready. The important question is, are you ready?"

Music has defined me since I was a small child growing up with ten brothers and sisters during the Great Depression. With no help from an alcoholic father, in struggling to take care of her family my mother somehow found fifty cents a week to cover piano lessons for one of her younger sons. I was a little guy. From the age of five I was always being hoisted onto tables to sing at our South Chicago YMCA. I won practically every talent contest and as a result was always defending myself against envious neighborhood tough guys. For high school graduation I surprised members of my wrestling team by performing the First Movement of Mendelssohn's G-minor Piano Concerto.

Before proceeding with this book I pondered how best to highlight the multi-layered aspects of a *Razz Ma Tazz* career. In struggling to feed my family I was compelled to navigate power struggles among directors, entertainers, and producers. At times I committed a few miscues in judgment and walked away from trouble when I should have stayed in the fight. Admittedly, I made some questionable (some say, gutsy) choices, was fired a couple of times.

Over the years I picked up a Director's Emmy for the daytime serial, *The Doctors,* and received three music awards from the American Society of Composers, Authors and Publishers. I wrote and recorded many television themes you are likely to have heard, and numerous songs you will be able to listen to as you read this book or visit my website. Among them is *Christmas Eve in My Home Town,* which the American Forces Network labeled, "The Soldier's Christmas Song." In later years I was an assistant director in a long line of movies including *Romancing the Stone, Bronco Billy,* and *Midnight Run,* as well as assisting my son, Billy Zabka (*Karate Kid, Back to School*) in producing his Oscar-nominated film, *MOST.*

In the writing of this book, of singular importance was my desire to credit my devoted wife and family for allowing me the freedom to follow my instincts and pursue my dreams. I suppose I encountered the problems of any author, that of selection. As I went along I heeded the voices of friends who admonished me to avoid the clichés of "and then I had lunch with," and "then I worked with so and so." Rather, I have attempted to include those in my personal and professional life who have been there for me, who have offered a step up along the way and kept me centered, for there have been many.

Billy offered this observation:

> *If there's a message in your story, Dad, it's what it means to be an American, to follow one's dreams, to take chances, to travel west in search of gold and some fools' gold, but at the end of the day to be able to come home to someone who loves you. The recognizable "names" in the book are fun wallpaper and provide a colorful, if not controversial canvas for the story. When all is said and done, the actual "star" in your story is the reader who walks with you on an amazing journey where victory lies in the power of love expressed in family that affirms one's purpose and keeps life in perspective.*

This is my story . . .

PART

I

The Making of a Man

BING CROSBY'S "HOLLYWOOD PALACE"

Kate Smith introducing her new yuletide recording

CHAPTER 1

Christmas Eve in My Home Town

Like the winds of the sea are the ways of fate as we journey through life.
'Tis the set of the soul that decides its goal, and not the calm or the strife.
—Ella Wheeler Wilcox

Following World War II it seemed that having finished college and pursued a career as songwriter, life would have returned to some semblance of normalcy. It didn't turn out that way. Anticipating a protracted period of reconstruction and peace, our country had dismantled most of its armed forces. In its wake, the U.S. became embroiled in a Cold War with Russia that was nearing the boiling point. To compound the issue, in 1951 the Korean War was one year old, and the possibility of a second, two-ocean war loomed high on the horizon. With only skeleton reserves at its disposal, the likelihood that unmarried veterans would be called back to active duty was both real and imminent.

1951 was also the year my first song was published. Don Upton and I wrote *Christmas Eve in My Home Town* when we were Page Boys for NBC in Rockefeller Center. I had no burning desire to return to the South Pacific, and joined an NBC Psychological Warfare Group bound for Europe.

Singing idol Eddie Fisher, then PFC Fisher, was entertaining our troops in Europe at the time. I had known Eddie as a civilian and had played some songs for him at NBC. When I met him again in Germany I approached him with American Forces Network Commander Colonel Philip Johnson to see if he would consider recording *Christmas Eve in My Home Town* for AFN. As a first published song, this project was priority for me. The rest is history. Eddie's recording caught on like wild fire. Over AFN in 1952 it became the most requested Christmas song in Europe.

In 1966, at the height of war in Vietnam, "Miss God Bless America," Kate Smith, recorded *Christmas Eve in My Home Town* and introduced it on Bing Crosby's *Hollywood Palace* television show and *The Johnny Carson Tonight Show*. In her discussion with Johnny she described how she sat down with me and taped thirty-six individual holiday messages for broadcast over AFN-Vietnam and its stations around the world, wherever our troops were stationed. Among the ships at sea receiving Kate's message were the aircraft carriers USS Oriskany, the USS Coral Sea, the USS Constellation, the USS Franklin D. Roosevelt, and the flagship USS Hornet.

My wife Nancy and I had extended families serving in Vietnam who heard Kate's message and recording over AFN. Two were pilots, another was a Green Beret, and the other was a sailor on a gunboat in the Mekong Delta. A video recording of Kate's visit with Johnny was aired over AFN-Vietnam as well, but I was told it was burned or otherwise destroyed along with other programs when Saigon fell. To my dismay I don't have a video copy of the interview. Due to extreme negligence on my part I failed to have one made and, unfortunately, the Kate Smith-Johnny Carson tribute was among the early *Carson Tonight* shows which NBC destroyed.

To view the Kate Smith-Bing Crosby video, go to www.zabka.com

Later in this book you will learn about Operation Desert Shield and Desert Storm, and how the Kate Smith-Johnny Carson interview was a major factor in our government granting permission for Christmas music to be broadcast to our troops in the Persian Gulf. Still later, in the Iraqi War, the broadcast continued to play a significant role in our Department of Defense's establishment of a full-blown American Forces Network broadcasting station in Baghdad.

To me, music is a blessing. It conjures up memories like no other medium. When I was overseas there were certain songs that created a bridge to home and to my country. In building lasting relationships and experiencing the ups and downs of camaraderie, I learned I could best communicate my emotions through song. Over a period of time music became the crucible of values that would shape the man I would become. Eventually, it would become my legacy. That is the unique power of song. Whenever I entertain folks in retirement and assisted living residences today, I find myself among kindred spirits. "Something old, something new, something borrowed, or something blue" is what they want to hear.

In 2007, Gary Bautell, Broadcast Director, phoned me from AFN headquarters in Frankfurt, Germany, to tell me the network had labeled *Christmas Eve in My Home Town* "The Soldier's Christmas Song." He went on to say that two special radio and television programs on its history with the Armed Forces would be fed by satellite to over 300,000 service members and their families in Europe, Korea, Japan, the Middle East, Iraq and Afghanistan, and Direct to Ship (DTS) to the Navy.

This special recognition by AFN sparked a long-standing interest to visit Camp Roberts where I had taken seventeen weeks basic training during World War II. Seven of my brothers and I served in that conflict, five of us winding up in California before being shipped overseas from the San Francisco Port of Embarkation. Whenever we could muster weekend passes we would get together, and Camp Roberts was one of our rendezvous spots. Back then it was the largest Army replacement depot in the country. Curiosity getting the best of me, I felt the time had come to check out my old stomping grounds.

From our home in Los Angeles my wife Nancy and I drove northward along the sea route before angling northeast onto King's Highway

101. The ocean drive was breathtaking, with waves crashing along the shore and surfers enjoying their sport. By contrast, the desert route toward Paso Robles where the camp was located appeared dull and uninteresting. All around us was dry, barren land, the only visible activity being an occasional jack rabbit scurrying across the sand.

After an hour or so a huge compound of buildings came into view, row upon row of sorry-looking, gray, wooden barracks in total disrepair. As we drew nearer to the entranceway we paused under a large, half-moon shaped sign, its paint blistered and peeling, its greeting discernible, nonetheless:

WELCOME TO CAMP ROBERTS

Driving past a dilapidated guard shack, Nancy eased our station wagon through the open gate and onto the facility, parked it near a building, and turned off the motor. The outside temperature was near boiling point. Under foot, weeds stretched boldly through wide cracks in the hot asphalt. During World War II this place was alive and buzzing with men and equipment. Half a million soldiers trained here. Now everything was quiet, a camp lost in time.

My memory bank went into overdrive as flashbacks of having soldiered here stirred a dozen emotions. Surveying the area, I recalled events of long ago. In a moment, as if shaking off a dream, imaginary sounds of a military band playing *Stars and Stripes* caused me to turn toward the parade ground where I envisioned platoons of men passing in review before a grandstand of officers and dignitaries.

An old sergeant barking orders to his men turned my head in another direction: "Right now we're going to police this area so clean you can eat off it. I want everything picked up. If you can't pick it up, plant it. If you can't plant it, paint it. If you can't paint it, salute it. All I want to see is asses and elbows. Move out!"

Down another street were remnants of a building no soldier cared to visit, the camp Dispensary, where a long line of soldiers were waiting to receive their battery of malaria and other shots. I was nineteen years old and had a burning desire to be a fighter pilot. Hearing that the nutrients from carrots would help strengthen my eyes I was forever chewing on the orange sticks. One or two were always protruding from my shirt pocket. I was the butt of everyone's jokes. During a barracks inspection one of my buddies hid some carrots in my foot locker where the inspecting officer could "accidently" discover them. I had been set up good and proper. Everyone enjoyed a good laugh until they learned that I had strengthened my vision to 20/15 in both eyes. To this day I do not wear glasses.

Time continued in reverse as my attention was drawn across the compound to the Enlisted Men's Club where I was seated at the piano. I had taken song writing seriously at this point and was working on a new tune when a sergeant approached me and ordered me to report to the company commander. Staring at my shirt pocket he then said, "and ditch the damn carrots."

I had no idea why the captain had sent for me. He seemed agitated as he returned my salute while shuffling through a stack of papers. "So you want to be a fighter pilot, do you, Private?" he asked. "Look what I have here: 'For Necessary Action.' 'For Necessary Action.' 'For Necessary Action.' What in the name of all hell did you do, Zabka, write to the President of the United States?"

Anticipating being put on KP duty for the remainder of the war I managed a weak, "Yes, sir."

"Yes. Well, guess what I have here, Private? Direct orders, all the way down from the Pentagon, instructing me to 'Transfer said Private to the Replacement Depot at Fort Ord, California, there to be placed on cadre assignment pending arrangements for said Private to proceed to the Presidio at Monterey, there to pursue Air Corps flight tests.'"

A mixture of happiness and disbelief crossed my face as the captain shook his head and, obviously displeased with my action, asked if the government directive was "quite satisfactory" to me?

"Yes, sir, it is, sir," I replied.

"Yes. Well, just for the record, Private, between you and me, this letter you wrote to the President, it's true, right? You didn't make this up? I mean, the Pentagon must've run a check on all this. There are five of you Zabka boys in the service, right?"

"Actually, there are six now, sir. Brother George has just been called up. He's on his way to Keesler Air Force base in Mississippi."

"And the other four brothers, where are they?"

"Frank, he's the oldest. He's in Europe with General Patton. Next is Brother Al. He's with the First Marine Division, on Guadalcanal."

The captain prodded me to continue. "John is next oldest, sir. He's with the 1112th Combat Engineers in New Guinea. A big push is on. His company is moving north."

"Just as a matter of curiosity, Private, how is it you seem to know where each of them is located, exactly?"

"We created kind of a code, sir, in our letters. It's been pretty accurate so far."

"And brother five: I presume he's next oldest. Where is he stationed?"

"That'd be Bob, sir. He transferred into Navy pilot training following the Sullivan incident. He claimed he'd had enough of hearing 'Taps' being played at Arlington Cemetery all day long."

"The 'Sullivan incident' . . . you're referring to the five Sullivan brothers?"

"Yes sir. Bob was attached to the department of the Navy that wrote letters to families of loved ones missing or killed in action. When the Sullivan boys went down with their ship Bob was assigned the task of writing to their parents. President Roosevelt signed the letter."

"Yes. Well . . ."

"Sir, about my writing to the President: I mean, the Sullivan boys wrote to him and they were allowed to serve on the same ship."

"They went down with it, too."

"I just want a plane, sir. I think I could be a good pilot."

"Yes. Well, it appears your family has some sort of pipeline to the White House. My orders are to give you a chance to get your plane. You are to be transferred to Fort Ord in Monterey, and be placed on work assignment until notified to proceed to the Presidio for flight tests.

After signing and initialing a stack of documents he handed them to me. "Give these to your sergeant. You might want to make a copy for your scrap book, if you ever survive this war. You're dismissed."

I had just reached the door when the captain stopped me with, "Good luck, Private. I hope you get your plane." And then he added, "and ditch the damn carrots!"

Brothers seven and eight (the twins, Clifton and Clifford) later entered the service. Clifton ("Hap," we called him) was a Lieutenant in the Corps of Engineers and Clifford ("Lucky") was a Navy Oral Surgeon. Had I realized the war was going to continue long enough for them to come in, I would have included their names when talking with my C.O.

After my verbal dressing down by the captain I was transferred to the replacement depot at Fort Ord. While there I was assigned to the Military Police guarding prisoners on company work detail and road marches. Sometimes we would bivouac overnight in the hills of Carmel. In the morning we would engage in target practice, shooting fifty caliber machine gun bullets at wind socks being towed over the water by fixed-wing aircraft.

One of my assignments at Fort Ord was to guard a private who was charged with dereliction of duty. With either a 45mm pistol or a carbine over my shoulder I walked ten paces behind him as he went about his chores. His name was Nathan Greenberg, a skinny kid from Brooklyn. It didn't seem like he could hurt a flea, but he had committed a serious offense, especially in time of war. He had fallen asleep on guard duty. The corporal of the guard reported him to the platoon sergeant. From there, Greenberg's case went to the platoon and company commanders and finally to the battalion commander who threw the book at him.

Greenberg was court marshaled, denied all pass privileges, and shipped overseas without a furlough or even the possibility of a family visit. It was a tough lesson, but it may have saved his life overseas, along with others.

Meanwhile, the time for my Air Corps tests at the Presidio at Monterey came and went. I didn't pass. I was never good at multiple choice questions. It would have been wiser if I had simply followed my basic instincts and selected obvious answers instead of analyzing each question to death. Having blown all chances of becoming a fighter pilot, I was truly devastated. Nevertheless, as disappointed as I was I came to believe the good Lord was watching out for me. Had I been given a plane I probably would have done something foolish with it and not be here today. I had to erase the subject from my mind. *You did all you could,* I said to myself. *It's time to move on.*

The Army offered me the opportunity to attend Officers Candidate School, but I declined. Being a fighter pilot, responsible for my own plane, my own destiny, was one thing; leading men into battle was another. I had no stomach for that. I resigned myself to being told where to go, what to do, what to eat, and when to sleep. At age nineteen it was my first lesson in choosing whether to lead or to follow. I would know soon enough whether or not my decision was a sound one.

Before shipping out I was granted a furlough and flew to Chicago to say goodbye to Mom, my three sisters, Marie, Sylvia, and Georgia, and the younger twins, Hap and Lucky. As I entered our apartment Mom was hanging her service pennant back in the window with a sixth star attached representing brother George's entry into the service.

Among a gallery of pictures on the piano was a photo of Sylvia's three little boys. Almost breaking the spell, Mom remarked, "I hate to say this, Sylvia, but I believe you are raising your sons to go to war." Sylvia's reply was, "Oh, Mom, don't be silly." But guess what? During Vietnam, two of them went in.

THE ZABKA BROTHERS IN WORLD WAR II

Frank *Al* *John*

Bob *Stan* *George*

Clifford *Clifton*

CHAPTER 2

On to the Islands

A journey of a thousand miles begins with a single step.

—La-tzu

In mid-June, 1943, I was on a troop ship bound for the South Pacific. We sailed a west-by-southwest course, eventually crossing the International Date Line. Our destination: Goodenough Island in the Solomon Sea, off the eastern coast of New Guinea. The Japanese occupied Goodenough after Pearl Harbor but were driven off by the Australians who built landing strips from which large and small aircraft could operate.

Ordinarily, an ocean crossing might take a week or more, depending on the weather and other conditions. Ours took thirty days as it was forced to zigzag through enemy waters to avoid detection by submarines. All garbage was weighted down and emptied into the sea in the evening. Under threat of severe penalty, the smoking lamp was out before nightfall, as the striking of a single match was detectable for miles.

Thirty days on a troopship is an eternity. You sweat a lot, especially in the confines of six-tiered bunks, smelly mess halls, and performing daily work routines. To keep us busy we would no sooner finish swabbing the decks when we were instructed to do it again. Newly issued fatigues were stiff and would smell raunchy when worn a few days. Instead of regular toilet soap we scrubbed our gear in the shower with non-lathering salt soap and a hand brush.

There is an army term, "field expedient." When a jeep, truck or piece of equipment would break down and there were no replacement parts, someone would contrive a means to keep it going, thus the term, "field expedient." As for washing our clothes, one bright GI had a brainstorm. He would take his fatigues topside, tie a line around them, and throw them overboard to be thrashed about in the waves. When he pulled up the line, his fatigues would be soft and smell fresh and clean. I thought it was a clever idea and I decided to do the same. The only difference was I threw my line overboard near a porthole on the ship where toilet waste was being dispensed. When I pulled up my line my fatigues seemed heavier than usual. Examining them further, guess what I found in the pockets? Not funny! I cut the line free with my bayonet, and for the rest of the voyage I had one remaining set of fatigues. I washed them in the shower the conventional way, with salt soap and a hand brush, and went around ship in shorts until they dried.

Because of a severe outbreak of typhus on Goodenough Island, our ship was forced to continue across the channel to a replacement depot at Milne Bay in the southern part of New Guinea. Brother John's 1112th Combat Engineers Company was further north in New Guinea, while brother Al's First Marine Division was on Guadalcanal. Maybe we'd catch up with each other one day and spend some time together. That was our hope.

Have you ever heard of "Tokyo Rose?" She was the Japanese radio personality who played American music from a studio in Japan. Her daily psychological warfare broadcasts were designed to lower morale and convince GIs that our loved ones back home were being unfaithful. The heartbreaker song she aired one day was, *Don't Cry, Joe, Let Her Go, Let Her Go, Let Her Go.* The words had special meaning for me because at mail call I received a Dear John letter from a girl I was serious about in California. While her brother was in the service we borrowed his convertible to go picnicking along the Monterey Peninsula. I hadn't been out of the States long enough to hiccup when I learned she married a GI photographer who was able to pull permanent stateside duty. I had written a song for her, *Just One of Those Things,* which was what our brief romance turned out to be.

One afternoon I returned from a work detail to find an army of jungle ants invading my duffle bag. Believe it or not, this incident upset me far more than the Dear John letter. Thousands of these pesky creatures had followed the sweet scent of chocolate and worked their way up, over, and down into the bag, chewing their way into a box of Heath candy bars I had just received from home.

Until we were assigned to a permanent outfit there was little to do at the replacement depot except to clean our weapons and exercise. To kill time, a couple of buddies and I would trek down to the ocean and watch landing barges unload men and supplies. One afternoon we noticed incoming troops chomping away on apples and oranges as they came ashore. The only fresh fruit available to us on the island were bananas and more bananas. Some replacements on these barges were enjoying ice cream, and the three of us wondered how long it would take to swim out to the mother ship and partake of some of those goodies.

It didn't appear to be anchored all that far from shore, perhaps a mile or so. We soon learned a hard lesson on the illusion of distance over a body of water. As it turned out, the ship was moored at least twice as far from land as we had estimated. We reasoned that if we pushed a log in front of us for an occasional rest we could reach the ship in about a half hour. Not so! Whenever we pushed the log forward a few feet, we'd fall back the same distance. To top it off, the weather changed dramatically and the ocean turned choppy. Rising waves slapped at our faces and the salty Pacific water burned our eyes.

Exhausted but victorious, we finally reached our destination and made our way up the long stairway at the stern of the ship. Reaching topside, we were met by three wiseacre marines. Their first words to us were, "How do you gentlemen intend to get back to shore?" We figured we would catch the next landing barge, except they told us the last one had gone in. They lied. After a strong reprimand, a ship's officer sent us ashore minus any fresh fruit or ice cream, or "whatever else you boys came looking for."

During our swim out to the troopship we swallowed enough salt water for an entire regiment. Thankfully, we had been provided ample fresh water to flush out our systems. Our supposedly easy, swimming-with-a-log ocean adventure had consumed all of three hours! MPs were waiting to return us to our unit. Our platoon sergeant, not at all pleased that we had left the area without permission, assigned us to KP duty as company punishment. That work detail did not last too long once I learned how to make wine. When opening cans of fruit I would save extra peach, apple, or other juices and pour the entire mixture into a bottle, add a touch of sugar and raisins, secure a piece of cloth over the top, and then let the mixture ferment overnight. Once my platoon sergeant tasted the heavenly brew I was his wine maker until I left the island.

A pass-the-time sporting event was going down to a swimming hole that had been carved out by a swift-running mountain stream. The water was always fresh and cold and was so clear you could place a shining object among the pebbles and rocks, go upstream, and then let the swift current carry you underwater as you searched to retrieve the object.

Sometimes we would climb up the side of the mountain and swing into the water from a rope. One of my buddies dared me to dive from a tree stump, increasing the diving distance by about three feet. Accepting the challenge, I recalled a movie in which movie star Alan Ladd did a perfect swan dive, his head turned upward, his arms pressed to his chest, ready to open. Before touching the water, Ladd tucked his chin into his chest, straightened his arms over his ears, and hit the water, barely creating a splash. It was a beautiful dive. I imitated him.

My dive felt good. I cut the water like a knife, but found myself struggling to re-surface. In an instant I was being pulled ashore by my colleagues, a two-inch gash oozing blood from my head. Besides the extra height of the dive, the water level had dropped considerably during the night, and I hit the bottom hard and fast. At the Dispensary a bandage filled with peroxide was attached to my skull until the wound healed. I have never had such a headache, before or since.

Before I could get into any more trouble, my transfer orders were cut and I left the New Guinea Replacement Depot to join an artillery battery across the channel on Bougainville.

THE BROTHERS GET TOGETHER

Pilot Bob. Left to right: John (kneeling), me (sitting), Bob (behind the ladder), Al (far right)

CHAPTER 3

Reunion in the Pacific

It is part of a good man to do great and noble deeds, though he risks everything.

—Plutarch

Bougainville is an island in the Solomons, north of Australia and to the east of Papua New Guinea. America's success at Bougainville isolated all Japanese forces and had a vital impact on the balance of naval power in the Central Pacific. In late November, 1943, the Japanese airfields on the island were neutralized by elements of the Third Marine Division. On December twenty-first it was replaced by the Army Division to which I was assigned as part of an anti-aircraft unit guarding the airfields. It was also Christmas time.

Not to be denied a yuletide celebration, my buddies and I decorated our tent fronts with white sand from the beach and painted sea shells and coconuts which we strung throughout the area as ornaments. One member of our group received a colorful ten-foot "Merry Christmas" banner sprinkled with fake snow. Even though it arrived in mid-January, it was of no consequence. It hung in our area for ten months, until we shipped out to the Philippines.

For a long while I lost track of my brother John until I learned his Combat Engineer Group had taken part in the Leyte landings in October, 1944. Meanwhile, brother Al's First Marine Division had wrapped up business on Guadalcanal before engaging in the Iwo Jima and Okinawa campaigns. Although we continued to crisscross the islands in this fashion, there was no opportunity for the three of us to get together. When we finally did, it was my brother Bob who made it happen.

Here is the story: When Franklin Roosevelt died on April 12, 1945, Harry Truman assumed the presidency. Shortly thereafter, following the Allied victory in Europe, Truman sent four-star Admiral Royal E. Ingersoll on a one-month mission to the South Pacific. As Pilot-Navigator of the admiral's C54 Flagship, Bob's assignment was to deliver him and his power group of dignitaries to every island they needed to visit. That is when he would rendezvous with his brothers.

There were six of us in the service at the time, three of us in the South Pacific. Our journeys began at these locations:

WAR TABLE, 1943			
John	San Francisco	to	New Guinea
Al	Los Angeles	to	Guadalcanal
Frank	New York	to	England
Stan	San Francisco	to	New Guinea
Bob	Oakland	to	St Mary's Pre-flight, San Francisco
George	Chicago	to	Keesler AFB, MS

As the families at home followed the action via victory letters (V-mail, we called them), the six of us changed locations:

WAR TABLE, 1944			
John	New Guinea	to	Leyte, Philippines
Al	Guadalcanal	to	Okinawa, Iwo Jima
Frank	England	to	Omaha Beach, France
Stan	New Guinea	to	Bougainville
Bob	Admiral's C54 Flagship	to	Prepping one-month South Pacific tour, San Francisco
George	Keesler Field	to	Lowry AFB, Denver

Although the war in Europe had ended, the war in the Pacific moved forward, and so did we:

WAR TABLE, 1945			
John	Leyte	to	Luzon, Philippines
Al	Iwo Jima	to	Guam
Frank	France	to	Italy/Germany
Stan	Bougainville	to	Leyte, Philippines
Bob	San Francisco	to	One-month South Pacific tour
George	Lowry AFB	to	Sheppard Field, TX

Before the admiral's journey to the Pacific got underway, brother Bob copied a letter to Al, John, and me in the Pacific. His closing remark, though purposely vague, offered a hint that something was brewing: "Wouldn't it be great if we could get together out there before too long?"

A follow-up letter from home offered this clue:

> *Bob phoned. He said I would not be hearing from him for awhile, that he was going away. If he knew the destination he would not, or could not say. I pray for his safety, and yours, all of you.*
> *Love, Mom*

Bob's reference to our "getting together before too long" soon became a reality. The first leg of the admiral's tour was a 4,224 mile flight from Oakland, California, to the naval base at Pearl Harbor. From there, following conferences and briefings in Hawaii, the big plane lifted off on a 3,820 mile flight to the island of Guam in the Mariana Islands, headquarters of Fleet Admiral Chester Nimitz.

Coincidentally, Al's "Blue Diamond" First Marine Division had just arrived on Guam for a rest period prior to going into Tientsin, China. The campaigns of Guadalcanal, Eastern New Guinea, New Britain, Iwo Jima and Okinawa behind them, his outfit was considered the most decorated unit of its size in the Marine Corps. The battle for Okinawa has been referred to as the "Typhoon of Steel" because of the intensity of the fighting. Lasting eighty-two days, from April to June of 1945, it was the largest amphibious assault in the Pacific War.

When Admiral Ingersoll's C54 Flagship landed on Guam, Bob wasted no time hunting down his older brother. Approaching a marine sorting out some gear, he asked where he might find Private First Class Al Zabka. Surveying the area, the young marine pointed and said, "That's him over there, sir, by that tent."

Gnawing away on a cigar stub, Al had embedded a broken piece of mirror into a bar of soap, anchored it onto a tent pole, and was carving away on a heavy growth of beard. He had almost finished shaving when he paused to gaze at a familiar face in the mirror.

"Would you like a fresh cigar?" Bob asked.

The only words Al could muster were, "Well, I'll be damned!"

"Mom was worried about you guys. She sent me out here to check on you."

Having been assured that he would maintain a low profile, Admiral Ingersoll gave Bob permission for Al to wear lieutenant insignia and live in the officers' quarters. Al enjoyed the luxury of sleeping under sheets, enjoying steaks and salads, smoking fresh cigars, and downing all the Cokes he could drink, with ice! To this day Bob says he can picture Al flushing toilets just to hear the sound. I asked Bob if this were true, and he assured me it was.

Five days on Guam provided sufficient time for the two to catch up on all the news, exchange stories, pitch horseshoes, and speculate as to what action might lie ahead in the Pacific. They talked until the wee hours of the morning, not so much about the war but about home and family. In and around Chicago Al was known as the "Harry James of the trumpet." His sixteen piece band, *Hal King and His Syncopators of Swing*, was very popular. When the band would rehearse at our house, neighborhood kids would always peer through the basement windows to watch.

Sometime in the conversation Al mentioned he had heard brother George was called up and had joined the Air Corps, and asked if brother Frank was still with Patton's Third Army Corps in Europe. Bob said the last he'd heard from Frank was that he had built a motorcycle out of spare parts, and that his captain had attempted to commandeer it. Frank was reluctant to relinquish his bike, but the officer argued that Frank was not authorized to have one. Without further discussion, Frank "accidentally" shifted his bike into gear and steered it into a brick wall, explaining that it was "a foreign bike, not to be trusted." I had always believed that Frank was a part of the Normandy invasion, but later learned his outfit joined Patton after the Omaha Beach landing.

Al and Bob's conversation on Guam shifted to the question of what the Admiral's mission in the Pacific was all about. Bob would say only that they didn't tell him, that he was just the pilot-navigator. The Philippines was on his itinerary, though, and he said he was hoping to hook up with John and me while there.

Finally, the time for parting had come. The admiral's business on Guam completed, Admiral Ingersoll and his party set out for Iwo Jima, Saipan, Okinawa, and then east to Luzon in the northern part of the Philippines. The Flagship had barely touched down on the tarmac when Bob high-tailed it out the cabin door and down the ramp, bound for the signal shed. Approaching the corporal on duty he inquired as to where the Sixth Division Combat Engineers was located.

"Sir, that's restricted information," was the reply.

"I appreciate that, corporal, but look," Bob said, "my brother's with the Sixth Engineers. I'm with the Flagship. Come on!"

Referring to a wall map of the Luzon area, the corporal pointed out John's location. "They're up here, sir, in the hills, chasing Yamashita."

Over field phones, Bob and John had a brief but spirited conversation. "How long are you going to be here, brother?"

"We leave tomorrow. It'd be great if you could join us for a few days. You will have to find your way back to Luzon, though."

"No problem. As soon as I can clear with my C.O., I'll be out of here. Watch for a cargo or recon plane."

Armed with two, back-to-back three-day passes, John arrived at the airstrip in a matter of hours. "You look pretty sharp, commander, all cleaned up and shiny. What's your next stop?"

"The Samar Naval Base, off Leyte. Stan's on Leyte."

"I know," John replied. "And I know Leyte. We made the landing there. How long are you going to be staying on Samar?"

"I am not sure. Three days is my guess. It's a major stopover point for the admiral, perhaps one of the last before heading home."

I was on anti-aircraft duty at the Leyte airstrip when I received a call from the switchboard operator at company headquarters: "Hey, Carrot, some sergeant named Rocky is on the phone. He's at the Tacloban air strip. Want to talk to him?"

"Yeah. Sure. It's my brother. His men nicknamed him Rocky because he always bedded them down in the rocks."

I wondered what John was doing on Leyte. I thought he was up north in Luzon. My C.O. seemed as pleased as I that he was here. Perhaps now he would get an update on what was actually happening up front. "Sir," I asked, "who's the fastest driver in the outfit?"

"Kulchisky," he said. "I'll send him."

In less than five minutes, PFC "Mad Stanley" Kulchisky, a crazy Polish kid from the Bronx, barreled into the area at full throttle. I hopped in his jeep while it was making its turn, and together we headed for the Tacloban airstrip.

Meeting up with my brother was a heady experience. It had been a few years since we last rendezvoused in California. No sooner had he jumped into the jeep when Kulchisky executed a fast hundred and eighty out of the airstrip, hell-bent-for-leather, double-clutching the gears like a racing driver. We didn't go a hundred feet when John tapped him on the shoulder and asked him to stop the jeep.

"Young man," he said, "no one is shooting at us. There is no need to hurry. My outfit happens to hold the record for being under more consecutive days of bombardment than any other in the Pacific. I'd hate like hell for someone to write home and say I got killed in a jeep accident."

I asked Rocky why he left the 1112th Combat Engineers, the outfit he trained with back in the States. He said he didn't leave it voluntarily, that he was transferred out after his group secured the landing strip on Sansapor. He told me how his platoon had bedded down for the night, and in the morning he discovered one of his men had been killed. It appears the young man had left his foxhole for some reason or other and a trigger-happy lieutenant shot him. Upon investigation John and another sergeant learned this lieutenant did not invoke the designated password, but fired indiscriminately. To save face of the officer, and most likely to save his own command, Rocky's senior officer stripped both John and the other sergeant of their rank and transferred them out of the 1112th. John's new outfit, the Sixth Combat Engineers, later was part of the invasion force that made thrusts into Luzon to capture General Yamashita, the infamous "Tiger of Manila."

The name of the young soldier that was killed was Charles Kilcolin. After the war, John and two other brothers and I traveled to Salem, Virginia, to visit the grandparents who had raised the boy. They had never been told the full story of how Charles died, only that he was "killed in action." They appreciated hearing the true facts. We visited the grandparents often after that, developing a friendship that lasted for many years. To this day, Rocky's invaluable lesson in sense of duty and honor, coupled with his innate compassion for others, became my standard and my guide.

We left my outfit on Leyte early the following morning and hitched a ride on a cargo plane bound for Samar. Bob was at the airstrip waiting for every plane, figuring we had to be on one of them. Admiral Ingersoll gave permission for John and me to don officer's insignia just as he had for brother Al on Guam, and from that time on we lived in the officer's quarters enjoying great food and drink. *No question about it,* we thought, *a Navy officer's life is so sweet!*

It was reminiscent time and we took advantage of it, exchanging stories and getting caught up on just about every subject imaginable. This was not like sharing stories over a beer in a local pub back home. We had not seen each other for years, and we drank in the moment with gusto. We talked about the war being over in Europe, about the twins, Hap and Lucky (Clifton and Clifford) who had received their reserve army and navy commissions, and of course the family at home, and what we planned to do after we were discharged.

There was no USO on the island of Samar, and no piano in the officer's club where we were gathered. Still, my brothers talked me into singing *I Ain't Got Nobody (and nobody cares for me),* a song I used to sing at our South Chicago YMCA when I was a kid. Watching us recount events and carry on, a lady officer commented, "You know, if we were not so far from home I would swear you boys were brothers."

Later, as we walked around the little village, I spotted a beat-up old piano in a native hut and asked the owner if I would be allowed to play it. Bob always said that if there was a piano around, I would find it. In high school I had learned a classical arrangement of *Silent Night* that began and ended with the sound of carillon bells, and that is what they wanted to hear, a Christmas song, no less, in the middle of the summer! "And don't forget to put the bells in," Bob reminded me. Even though some keys were broken and some did not work at all, it felt good to play that old piano. Filipinos watched the proceedings through open, thatched windows of the hut, and as we left they presented us with baskets of fruit and nuts.

Time turned the pages, and all too soon the sleek, silver Flagship was rolled onto the runway. In an instant its powerful engines lifted it over the palm trees and into the morning mist. Watching the plane disappear I realized you did not have to be a thousand miles from home to appreciate the value of family or yearn for the sight of a familiar face. Whether one is near or far away, the feeling is the same. I make no apologies in saying the bond I shared with my family contributed to making me the man I would become. I learned another lesson, the value of life itself. Of the eight of us, three of my older brothers (Frank, Al, and John) were in the thick of things, while my outfit was always in the rear echelon mopping up. I would have changed places with either one of them in a minute, but by the grace of God we all came home in one piece. In the end, that is all that mattered.

As Bob's plane disappeared over the horizon Rocky and I figured the Admiral's final stops would be New Zealand, a debriefing at Fleet Headquarters on Guam, and (following some aloha time in Hawaii) they would be back in the good old USA. That was our guess, anyway. Actually, we learned that after the Samar briefings they flew to Hollandia, Guadalcanal, Australia, Samoa, Honolulu, Oakland, and then to Washington, D.C. In one month they had covered a total of 33,995 miles.

Rocky and I needed to get back to our units. He was able to hitch a ride on a cargo plane bound for Luzon. The trouble was, he had to help load it with metal landing strips, a job that took four hours to complete. He said the flight back was far from being comfortable as he had to sit atop banging and clanging (and sometimes shifting) sheet metal, quite a change from his cushy seat in the Flagship.

It took two days for me to get back to my outfit, as no cargo or other planes were bound for Leyte. Most were heading north where the action was. Eventually, I was able to hitch a ride on an oil tanker on its way across the channel. Mad Stanley picked me up at the boat docks in Tacloban, screeching his jeep out of the area once again like there was no tomorrow.

The question on our minds was what the admiral's South Pacific tour was all about. The Flagship was loaded with top military and civilian brass including Vice Admiral Ross McIntire (President Roosevelt's physician), and Secretary of the Navy, Struve Hensel. The fact is, barely two months after their trip, August sixth and ninth, two super bombs were dropped on Hiroshima and Nagasaki.

At our gun site on Leyte, a buddy and I were listening to the jungle network radio when we heard the announcement everyone had been waiting for:

> *. . . and thus the atomic bomb has written finish to the war in the Pacific. Today, September second, 1945, nearly four years after the bombing of Pearl Harbor and nearly four months after Germany's surrender in Europe, General Douglas MacArthur has accepted the Japanese surrender aboard the US Battleship Missouri in Tokyo Bay. World War II is over.*

MOM AND ELEVEN OF HER TWELVE CHILDREN

Front row: Marie, Mom Zabka, Georgia
Back row: Clifford, George, me, Bob (hidden), Sylvia, Clifton, Al, Frank, John

CHAPTER 4

Prelude to a Passion

Home is where the heart is.

—Pliny the Elder

There were two endings to World War II, victory in Europe (VE Day), and victory in Japan (VJ Day). The war in Europe began with the invasion of Poland on September first, 1939, and ended May eighth, 1945, four months shy of six years. The war in the Pacific began with the bombing of Pearl Harbor on December seventh, 1941, and ended on September second, 1945, three months shy of four years.

It was time to go home. As long as we made it back by Christmas, all that mattered to my buddies and me was that our names would be on the manifest of one of the next boats leaving the Philippines. The military point system dictating the order of our rotation to the States was calculated by a complicated evaluation process based on time in service, overseas time, and the theater of operation in which one served. If there were other conditions, it didn't matter a hill of beans to me or my buddies. The Army was going to do what it had to do anyway, so we figured we might as well relax and await the outcome.

My ship was part of a three-boat convoy. We were about a day out when loud speakers bellowed out this announcement, "Now hear this. Now hear this. The chaplain is looking for someone to play the organ during worship service. Anyone wishing to volunteer is requested to report to the duty officer on quarter deck." Before the announcement ended I was ushered into the chaplain's office and got the job. Except for setting up the room for chapel and passing out hymn books, playing the organ for church service was all I was required to do.

One afternoon while standing at the ship's railing I observed a spectacle too amazing to believe. From one of the ships in our convoy all manner of equipment was being pushed overboard: trucks, jeeps, Red Cross vehicles, weapons carriers, boxes filled with mess gear and other kitchen utensils, anything that would sink. Joining me topside was my chaplain. After watching all this for awhile he turned to me and offered this observation: "Son," he said, "You are now witnessing the waste of government in action, a hastily administered implementation of a needless job-creation technique."

To fill the void in our crossing and perhaps to help prepare us for return to civilian life, the chaplain held regular civilian rehabilitation classes. One of his techniques was to encourage group discussion on family values and how they had influenced our lives, especially in our formative years. Eventually it was my turn to address the group and since most activity in our house centered on my mother, it was about her that I addressed my thoughts.

Mom was a fixture in both elementary and high schools, always attending Parent Teacher Association meetings or volunteering her time on one committee or another. With a family of eleven, a Zabka was either entering a school or leaving one. After dinner one evening Mom dropped the hint that my high school principal would be delighted if I would play the piano for graduation. I didn't know what to say. It was okay to play an instrument in the school marching band or to be on a sports team, but for some reason playing the piano was considered a sissy thing, and so I never did. It didn't make sense, I suppose, but in the South Chicago neighborhood where I grew up that's the way it was, and I just wanted to be one of the boys.

As a special favor to my mother I agreed to play for graduation. After all, she did manage to put aside piano lesson money for me dating back to *The Great Depression* years; the least I could do was to show my appreciation. To prepare for the performance I set aside all activities and practiced the piano four hours a day for a solid month until I had memorized eighteen pages of the *First Movement of Mendelssohn's G-minor Piano Concerto.*

Bowen High is remembered as the school that famous drummer Gene Krupa attended. My graduating class was so big (over three hundred students) that it was necessary for the ceremonies to be held across town at Calumet High. The auditorium was huge, like the Radio City Music Hall in New York, with two balconies. I was seated by the steps leading up to the stage where the principal and other speakers were assembled. As a long Steinway grand piano was being rolled onto the stage a girl classmate seated next to me asked, "Who is going to play that thing?" I told her I was, and asked her if she would please help me off with my robe. She said she never knew I played the piano. "Nobody does," I said, "except my family." I stared at the Steinway for a long time before gathering enough courage to ascend the stairs. My fingers were loose, like rubber bands, ready! I felt I would get through the performance if my head and my hands cooperated.

My teacher was seated at the second piano in the orchestra pit, prepared to play the orchestral accompaniment. I don't believe I have ever been so scared. My hands were wet, and I opened and closed them for exercise. Looking out at the audience I saw my mother seated in the front row and stared at that place for the longest time before beginning to play. The school principal must have sensed my obvious stage fright because he leaned over to me with some encouraging words: "You're going to do just fine," he said.

Easy for him to say! My teacher simply waited patiently for me to begin. It seemed like an eternity, but before I realized it the moment had passed. The presentation was over. It really wasn't so bad after all. My buddies from the wrestling team were surprised to see me play the piano, but afterwards they said they enjoyed it, as did Mom and my family (of course!). I had done a lot of acting and singing since I was a kid, but this event was different, a defining moment for me. Little did I realize music would play so important a role in my life.

With high school and the graduation performance behind me, college loomed around the corner. My piano teacher's brother had earned his tuition money as a Red Cap at Chicago's Union Station, and I was encouraged to check it out. When I went for an interview the station master said he would hire me, except that I was too small. He was correct in one sense, as I weighed in at a mere one hundred fifteen pounds. When I explained what the station master told me, my mom suggested I write a letter saying I was a wrestling champ, and that I could wrestle luggage as well as any of the old timers on his staff. That is what I did, and that is how I got the job.

The following week I began hustling bags and wheeling luggage carts around the station and taxi stand. At the end of a day I was given one and a quarter cents for every bag I tagged. Union Station kept the larger hunk, eight and three quarter cents. But I did okay because I was able to keep all my tips. I especially watched for ladies with children, as they were very generous, as were sports teams. Sports teams tipped especially well. By the end of the summer I earned enough money to register at the University of Illinois for a year. The downside was that my piano hands became tough as iron. Even my calluses had calluses.

In the rehabilitation class aboard ship our chaplain asked why I talked about my mother, but not my dad. The reason I hadn't mentioned him, I explained, was because he was not a positive influence in my life. I never knew him in my growing-up years. When I asked my mom to tell me about him she said her greatest mistake was early in their marriage when she agreed to sell their beautiful one-acre home in Omaha to buy a small saloon and bowling alley in Prague, Nebraska. She said dad was a good accountant and eventually purchased some acreage next to their property, but when times went sour and money was scarce they lost everything. Dad also was a popular stage director and musician in Prague. Mom said he was a very proud man who neither drank nor smoked when they first married, but when he was unable to meet his financial obligations his pride got the best of him and he sought refuge in alcohol.

Their first half dozen children were born in Omaha and Prague: Marie, Frank, Sylvia, Al, John and Victor. Soon after Victor was born times got bad and they moved their family to Des Moines, Iowa, where Bob and I were born. Victor was just thirteen months old when the family doctor over-injected him with medicine for Diphtheria. He died in my father's arms. Grieving over his death, believing he should not have allowed the doctor such freedom of action, he took to drinking more and more.

A whiz at figures, dad found accounting jobs. Mom said that instead of money, sometimes he would be paid in material things like a Maytag washing machine. Occasionally a client would slip him a bottle of whiskey which he would hide from my mother.

In 1926, promising to straighten out and feeling he could earn a better living in Illinois, they moved their seven-member family to the steel mill district of South Chicago. For three years dad held his own until the stock market crash of 1929 triggered *The Great Depression* and long lines of unemployed. That's when my dad began drinking again. When he could find a job he wasn't able to hold on to it. I was only five years old at the time, unable to comprehend the seriousness of what was happening around me. It was during this ten-year period of extreme poverty that Mom gave birth to two sets of twins, George and Georgia and Clifton and Clifford.

A financial break came when the Internal Revenue Service paid my dad four hundred dollars a month to examine tax returns. Mom said he worked long into the night to earn overtime pay, and to stay awake he took to drinking more and more until she was powerless to stop it. She said it was the bad liquor of the *Prohibition* that ultimately did him in. Little by little the disease robbed him of a decent quality of life. His pride and self-esteem were the first to go. After that he lost complete control of his family and his ability to provide for it.

During these hard times everyone in the family pitched in and did what they could. Frank found work as a night watchman at Richie's Box Factory. Marie found a job at the telephone company and was able to get Sylvia part-time work as a switchboard operator. Al and John loaded boxes at Link Belt, a maker of farm tools. Bob had a paper route during the week and made extra money delivering milk on weekends. Whoever could find work put their earnings into the family pot. Mom handled the money. Whichever creditor knocked loudest at the door was the first to be paid.

The extent of Mom's devotion to my dad was commendable, if incomprehensible. Although encouraged by outsiders, she never put him out. "You don't know him like I do, she would say. He is not the man I married." Instead, she prepared a cot in the cellar for him to sleep and a place to put his belongings. The basement sink became his toilet. While in a drunken stupor, throughout the night he would direct his invective rhetoric at Mom with the foulest Czech words imaginable.

His downward spiral must have been difficult for my older siblings to witness, as they knew him in the early days when he was a good father and a responsible breadwinner. As a youngster, I feared him. If I was alone when he came upstairs to eat I would lock the basement door, pretending I wasn't home. "I know you're in there, Stanley," he would cry out. "Open this door!"

Brother John offered this perspective in his memoir: "Some are happy drinkers; some become drowsy and sleep off the booze; some become talkative; others become quiet and remorseful. Dad was abusive, both physically and verbally. He would lash out with his fists and utter words of unbelievable profanity. Yet there were times when he was a completely different man, quiet, somewhat conversant, and prone to go his own way and do his own thing around the house."

Twice the family checked dad into a rehab center to dry out, but always he begged to be brought home, declaring he was a different man, that he had changed. At any given time a neighbor might knock at our door to tell us Dad was lying in the prairie, and that maybe someone should go get him and bring him home.

Looking at my watch aboard ship I couldn't believe I had rattled on for so long. It seemed as though I had been talking for hours. When I finished my discourse the chaplain closed our group rehab session with the sage observation that for anyone who has not lived through *The Great Depression,* it would be wise to investigate what it took to survive that most egregious period in our nation's history.

I knew I wanted to make music my career, but I still had not settled on which college to attend. I preferred a small school, one that offered good music and communications curriculums. After being in the islands for so long the ice carnivals of Dartmouth College were especially inviting until I learned the school was a full day's journey from Chicago, too far from home for a holiday or a visit. Worse, I learned Dartmouth was an all-male school. I passed.

Once home I found it difficult re-adjusting to civilian life. Psychological barriers, real or imagined, clouded my mind. I found myself lost in a world in which I wasn't sure I belonged. The military had supplied years of direction and clear

MOM ZABKA'S LEGACY, 1986 REUNION

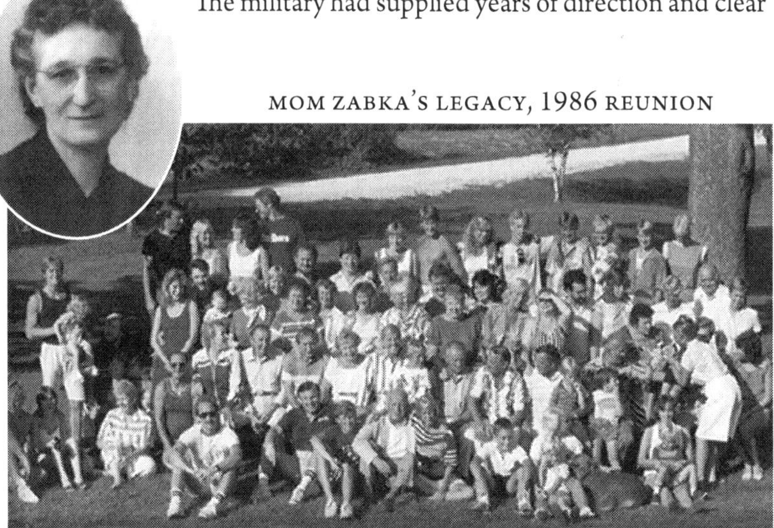

focus, replacing my own initiative to the point that now, without specific directives, ordinary tasks became a huge challenge. I became preoccupied with trying to understand who I was and what I should do with the rest of my life. Where a problem never existed, too often I invented one.

I don't believe I was suffering with what we now recognize as *Post Traumatic Stress Disorder*, a condition facing many of today's returning veterans. I just seemed to be mixed up like some of my buddies on street corners holding up lamp posts. At one point one of my closest friends suggested to my mom that I see a doctor, a notion my pride would not allow me to consider.

I found myself wrestling with the question of what the war was all about. So many lives and so much valuable time was lost and sacrificed, and for what? I looked for blame, trying to figure out who was at fault. I questioned if we were the ones called upon to right the wrongs of the world, and if so did we create more wrongs in our pursuit? How much were we willing to forgive and forget what we knew, or did not know, about what happened? Can we simply move on and build a new life, leaving these questions unanswered?

The further I delved into this reflection, the more isolated I became. What eventually became clear to me was that in searching for answers to these questions I had retreated into myself and was closing out the voices of loved ones who cared about me. Eventually I reasoned my problems were not so formidable that they could not be solved by adjusting my attitude, as simplistic as that may seem.

During this time there was an occasion when my older brother Frank chose to give John and me a verbal dressing down. Since he had returned from Europe Frank had not been able to sort out his pre-war marital problems with his former wife. They finally reconciled their differences and remarried, but until then Frank sought temporary escape in a local gin mill. A bit tipsy, he entered the living room of my mom's apartment to find John and me in a heated discussion about one thing or another. In no uncertain terms he let it be known that whatever was eating us was not so bad, and that we should back off a little and relax. Then he put his arms around us and in somewhat slurring words said: "You and Johnny, you guys have changed. You have become hard. You don't have to be hard, guys, come on."

Frank had made a good point. I needed to straighten myself out.

Most veterans, witness to more of the inhumane side of man's nature than they cared to remember, their dog tags tucked away in a drawer somewhere, were now checking the classifieds. Others, like me, grateful for the benefits of the GI Bill, were eager to finish their education.

Prior to the war I had completed a year at the University of Illinois, but having no desire to return to a large school I tagged along with a couple of buddies who were checking out a small Liberal Arts college within a reasonable driving distance from Chicago. DePauw University in Greencastle, Indiana, boasted of having excellent music and communications departments, plus its own campus radio station. Especially important was the fact that entrance exams for returning vets had been waived, as the school needed to replenish its monetary war chest. Definitely not going unnoticed was the welcome sight of girls wearing dresses and skirts.

DEPAUW UNIVERSITY

Me broadcasting the news over college radio

Singing at a Sigma Nu Jam session

As was true of most post-war fraternities on campus, the Sigma Nu fraternity house where I lived adhered to a no-nonsense academic policy. Its membership consisted mostly of returning vets who did not take to hazing or other frivolities they might have sanctioned at a younger age. Having been given the opportunity to pursue our education through the GI Bill, we felt we needed to honor that gift. DePauw did not allow cars and drinking on campus. I waited tables at the Kappa Kappa Gamma sorority house. Before returning to class some of us would gather around the piano to sing, and I created this little song for them:

THE KKG SONG

Gee, KKG . . .
You know you mean the world to me.
And gee, K-K-G . . .
You wear a pretty golden key.
When college days are through
I don't know what I'm gonna do,
Don't know what I'd do without you
Sink or swim I'll never doubt you
'Cause you know I love you, K-K-G.

Although I promised myself I would not get involved with anyone special, bingo, "Miss Wonderful" came into my life. We met in a local book store, struck up a conversation, began dating, and before I knew it things got serious. She ran for Campus Queen, but when she wasn't awarded the crown I told her not to feel bad because she was still a princess. That clever observation probably earned me a few brownie points, especially with her parents with whom we would dine when they visited her on campus. We were a fun couple, carefree and full of dreams, soaking up all the adventures college life might offer. As our sophomore year came to a close the love bug had bit me hard and I gave Miss Wonderful my fraternity pin. That's serious stuff in college; next to becoming engaged it's considered a strong commitment.

Although we lived in nearby Chicago neighborhoods I wasn't able to spend much time with her during our summer vacation as I learned that sixteen hours of science credits from my pre-war year at the University of Illinois weren't transferable to DePauw. As a consequence I had to travel to Northwestern University on Chicago's far north side to make up the credits by taking radio courses. I missed not seeing Miss Wonderful on a regular basis, but there was nothing I could do about it. When we returned to DePauw for our junior year, our budding romance had faded. Actually, it died. Over the summer months she fell for someone else. I believe her mother encouraged the breakup because of my large family. I think she was concerned that if we got married she wouldn't see much of her daughter. As it turns out, that "someone else" turned out to be her brother's war buddy who Miss Wonderful later married. To make it nice and cozy they set up housekeeping in an apartment upstairs from her mother and father!

Call it puppy love, first-time love, whatever you will, but my breakup with Miss Wonderful left me totally devastated. I think being jilted must be one of life's most painful experiences. It takes a long time to heal a broken heart, and I don't think it ever gets any easier. It wasn't a lesson I particularly cared to learn, but in retrospect it was probably a lesson in love that was helpful in my songwriting endeavors.

I needed to get my head back on straight, get focused, and develop a plan to move forward. One thing I promised myself, I absolutely would not get serious with anyone again. There would be no more romantic, time-absorbing entanglements, at least not until I graduated and could get going with my music career. On my return to DePauw for my junior year I used the title of a popular children's game to characterize a blues song I dedicated to Miss Wonderful for messing around with my heart:

TINKERTOYS ©

I tried to love you baby, but you went away,
I tried to show I need you but you just wouldn't stay,
This love we got'll go to pot, oh please come back.

I need-ya, I need-ya,
Get back on the track.

(Chorus)

I wanna love you, baby, love you much,
I wanna love you 'till you think that
heaven's close enough to touch,
Where are ya hidin'? Where are ya hidin'?
Put down those Tinkertoys
And take this lovin' from me.

No sense in runnin' around and doin' the town,
And thinkin' you're wise,
That ain't no way at all.
You're killin' the spark you put in my heart,
Why not let it be?
Shucks I'm the guy who calls ya, ev'ry night I'm free.

Now, there are times when I'm happy,
Times when I'm sad,
And there are times I want you near me
but you're nowhere to be had,
What is your trouble?
What is your trouble?
Put down those Tinkertoys,
And take this lovin' from me.

Many on campus believed *Tinkertoys* would be a great song for Nat King Cole, and so to interest the popular recording star I developed a plan. Whenever possible I rolled a piano into campus dining rooms and performed *Tinkertoys* for the students. I always came prepared with post cards requesting Nat Cole consider recording the song, and asked the students to please sign them and have them returned to me at the Sigma Nu house. I had obtained Cole's itinerary from a booking agent.

When Nat wasn't in a recording studio he was always on the road, and his travel schedule was consistently full. No matter. Wherever he entertained around the country a stack of postcards and a copy of the song awaited him.

My junior year turned out to be very productive, adding validity to my choice of Liberal Arts as a career goal. With music as my major and speech as a minor, I became active in many theatrical productions and entertained at all sorts of campus functions. DePauw's radio station, WIRE, was gaining in popularity and after being made its Student Director, I was awarded a coveted five hundred dollar radio scholarship from Eugene C. Pulliam, owner of the *Indianapolis Star* newspaper.

Towards the end of my junior year I broke my standing rule about entering another relationship and began dating "Miss Wonderful Number Two," a girl who lived in the sorority house where I was waiting tables. When I was offered a summer job in Hollywood I felt it was a good chance to get away for three months and see if this romance would survive longer than the previous one.

Monetary assistance from my family enabled me to purchase a used convertible for all of six-hundred dollars and I set out for California to be a Page Boy at CBS. My job was simply to usher guests in and out of its radio shows. I felt like a movie star as I parked my sleek, gunmetal grey Mercury in front of the studio on Sunset Boulevard. On one occasion, mistaking me for the actor Alan Ladd, someone asked me for my autograph.

Some of CBS's broadcasts drew huge crowds. People formed long lines and waited for hours to get a glimpse of their favorite idols. Movie star Mickey Rooney was one of the favorites at the time. His variety show and the Art Linkletter *Queen For a Day* broadcast originated from the Palladium Theater on Sunset Boulevard. I was assigned to these shows on a regular basis.

Movie actor Herbert Marshall starred in *The Man Called X*, a radio series broadcast from a CBS studio on Hollywood and Vine. He was the first movie star I had ever met. One day Mr. Marshall asked if I would arrange for some of his guests to view his show from the studio observation booth. As he walked away I noticed he was limping and asked if he had an accident. "Oh no, Stan," he said, "This is a permanent deficiency, World War I." Then he went on to say, "When I work in movies they give me parts where I don't have to move around very much. Thanks for asking, though." Mr. Marshall was a leading man in movies. I imagined that choosing roles for an actor with an uncontrollable limp was a big consideration for film makers.

Later in my career I was an assistant director on one of his films, *MacArthur*, starring Henry Fonda, in which Mr. Marshall played President Truman. On the film he seemed content biding his time in his dressing room or trailer until called to the set. Not so Henry Fonda, who always seemed restless. I remember waiting for instructions to bring him onto the set at our Burbank Airport location. Impatient with the slow pace of the filming, Fonda turned to me and said, "Stan, can't we get this company moving? If not, I'm going home." He would have, too. He had a short fuse.

During my off-duty hours I mingled with other movie royalty at the home of one of my college buddies, Frank Fowler. Frank was a part-time Hollywood stunt man who demonstrated to students how fights were staged in the movies. His step-sister was actress Barrie Chase whose father, Borden Chase, was a noted screen writer who worked on some of the Fred Astaire movies. Whenever I had time I would drive to the Chases' impressive home in swank Beverly Hills and lounge around the pool. Movie people were always there, gabbing, chasing a beer or cocktail, exchanging stories, reading a script. I had no agenda. I just thought it was cool to be there and soak up some rays.

Meanwhile, Miss Wonderful Number Two and her parents caught me off guard by paying me a surprise visit. They said that they were just passing through Los Angeles, but I believe her folks just wanted to check me out. I got the feeling her mom wasn't all too anxious for her only child to take up with someone from a large family pursuing show business as a career, especially a would-be songwriter. *Here we go again,* I thought!

After she and her parents said their goodbyes and returned to Indiana, I paid a visit to Nat King Cole who was appearing at Ciros, a popular Hollywood night spot. When he finished his set I introduced myself as the writer of *Tinkertoys* and the person responsible for all the postcards he received about recording the song.

"Yes," he said, "I know the song, I like it. It's a blues song, twelve bars to a phrase. Your middle phrase is eight bars. It should be twelve. But it's a good song. Is it okay if I make some changes?" I saw Nat twice after that, once at the Chicago Theater and later at the Copacabana in New York. On both occasions I was left with the feeling he would record the song, but it never happened.

When I returned to DePauw for my senior year I learned that a former fraternity brother was a vice president of RCA Records and sent him a copy and demo recording of *Tinkertoys.* His response was the song wasn't the caliber of material he would expect from a DePauw student, and that I should send him something like *Trolley Song* or *Stardust.* I was beginning to dislike rejection of any kind. I had a feeling it would not be the last I would receive in my career.

Meanwhile, back at school for our senior year Miss Wonderful Number Two was elected campus queen, and my vow not to get serious about anyone for awhile was put aside. We began dating on a regular basis, our time together gradually assuming serious proportions. My piano professor gave me a key to his private studio where I could write and practice the piano undisturbed, but it didn't always work out that way. Her sorority house was just across the street from the music building. Oftentimes she would bring her studies and join me in the studio. Given the advantages of so secluded a rendezvous spot, it was not easy for either of us to concentrate on school work.

We had another hideaway. Since cars were not permitted on campus I parked my Mercury convertible on Observatory Hill where married couples lived and cars were allowed. In the autumn when the leaves were turning color Miss Wonderful Number Two and I would sneak away to Indianapolis or drive to scenic spots in nearby Brown County. What made me believe time or space or sundials had anything to do with controlling the love bug is beyond me. In a romantic frame of mind, I removed my fraternity pin and offered it to her.

Totally smitten once again, I wrote a song for my Sigma Nu girl that later came close to being published. I now own all publishing rights and recorded the song in Paris with a string orchestra:

WONDRIN' AND DREAMIN' ©

Wondrin' and Dreamin'
Only Wondrin' only Dreamin',
Wondrin', will my secret dream come true?
Will I have you?

Wondrin' and Dreamin'
Only Wondrin', only Dreamin',
Tell me, do you wonder and dream like I do?

Will we build our dreams together?
Mine seem so empty when I'm sleepin' and
I'm dreamin' all alone.
Could there be a love more tender,
Or is this all so real because we share
a treasure no one's known?

(There's a million things that I'm)

Wondrin' and Dreamin'
Only Wondrin', only Dreamin',
Tell me, do you wonder and dream like I do?
Will I spend all my lifetime with you?

On graduation eve, the twelfth of June, 1949, we became engaged. Anxious to get moving with my career I was convinced that if I intended to be a songwriter, New York was where I had to be, and my fiancé felt the same way. The sooner I got started, the better. A fraternity brother's dad had a connection with an NBC vice-president, and so I knew I had a job waiting for me.

There were alternative plans. Since I had a taste of network radio in Hollywood I would explore announcing or directing or news writing in Manhattan. Television was showing signs of growth as well, and that industry particularly struck my fancy. There was an excellent television workshop in Manhattan. I planned to attend it in my spare time.

I was nearing my twenty-fifth birthday. If my music endeavors in New York did not work out I intended to return home, get a job in a local radio or television station, and raise a family. Promising to keep in touch and return to see her as often as possible, after a long embrace I said goodbye to my fiancé and boarded a night train to Manhattan. I was in for a big surprise. I did not realize a third uniform awaited me.

PART

II

The Making of a Musician

PAGE BOY DAYS AT NBC

Me, Dinah Shore, Martha Lou Harp, Henry Levine

CHAPTER

Broadway and the Music Beat

The difference between the almost right word and the right word, it's the difference between the Lightning Bug and the lightning.

—Mark Twain

Because I had been director of my college station and received a coveted radio scholarship, I was hoping I might be given a startup job in the newsroom or in NBC's music-variety division. Instead, I was offered a Page Boy job taking people on tour of television studios. The job paid only thirty-five dollars a week, but at least it got me in the door and that was important. Actually, it turned out for the better as not having a production job I had more free time to concentrate on my music. NBC had dozens of broadcast studios, most of which had a piano, and I found an ideal hideaway where I could write undisturbed. When not conducting tours I looked for opportunities to pitch my songs.

Most Broadway publishers had offices in an area of Times Square known as *Tin Pan Alley*. Former boxing great Jack Dempsey owned a restaurant on the main floor of the Brill Building where many authors and composers would gather and exchange stories. Every once in a while I would get a glimpse of some big-gun writers like Harry Warren, Bob Sour, or Johnny Mercer. Back then publishers maintained an open door policy for songwriters providing they didn't mind waiting in the hallway for hours on end. To be able to see any of the so-called Big-Three publishers (Universal, Sony, and Warner Brothers), a songwriter generally needed an inside connection.

I wondered where the term *Tin Pan Alley* had originated. Later I discovered that as publishers' pianos poured out tunes day and night, the cacophony of sound emanating from so many of them at the same time was like a symphony of tin pans being clashed together. The term has survived the test of time, although today we seldom hear pianos, only the click of keyboards and computer buttons and (very) loud speaker systems.

Meredith Willson was music director of NBC's *The Big Show,* the last radio extravaganza before television took over. Its director was Dee Engelbach, a former NBC Page Boy who took me on as his apprentice-assistant. Meredith wrote the show's well-known theme, *May The Good Lord Bless and Keep You.* On any weekly broadcast guest artists like Jimmy Durante, Bob Hope, Perry Como, Ethel Merman, and Jack Benny would alternate by singing a line or two.

When chatting with Meredith about his music exploits I asked him about his successful play *The Music Man* which launched the career of many fine artists and produced his memorable song, *Seventy-six Trombones.* Meredith explained that it had been a very hard sell. He said it took seven years for him to find enough backers to bring his play to the Broadway stage. This was the kind of persistence I would need in order to be a success in the music business.

We broadcast *The Big Show* from the *Center Theater* across the street from NBC. Mrs. Willson simply adored her talented husband. During rehearsal breaks she would sometimes drape a black cloak over his shoulders, "So he won't catch his death of cold," she would say. When I left the show to return to military service, Dee, Meredith and the show's star, Tallulah Bankhead, presented me with an autographed picture. I still have that treasured memento of the golden days of radio. It occupies a special place in my book of fond memories.

No artist more definably influenced my songwriting endeavors than composer-pianist-band leader, Duke Ellington. Whenever possible I would attend his sacred music concerts at New York's Fifth Avenue Presbyterian Church. I was often privileged to attend his band rehearsals and observe exchanges of musical forms and ideas with his co-writer and arranger, Billy Strayhorn who wrote Duke's orchestral theme *Take the A Train*. From swing to choral music to contemporary music, they covered it all. Together they wrote the jazz classic, *Satin Doll* to which Johnny Mercer wrote the lyric. Being a newcomer in the business, I learned a lot watching these giants at work.

Duke was totally wedded to his craft. His love for music was equaled only by his dedication to the art and his pursuit of perfection. It's said Ellington never took a break, that being on the road with his band 365 days a year was his vacation. I don't believe he traveled just to keep busy or to impress others with his dogged work ethic. Rather I believe there was a spiritual side of the man that longed for expression, and to that end he committed his God-given talents. French novelist Victor Hugo (*Les Miserables, Hunchback of Notre Dame*) best expressed the trust required in pursuing so noble an effort:

Let us be like a bird, for a moment perched
On a frail branch while he sings.
He feels it bend, but he sings his song,
For he knows that he has wings.

It was a year and a half before my first song was published. During that time I was acutely aware of the fact that songs went in and out of vogue depending on popular culture. At any one time ballads might be climbing the charts; at another time novelty songs would gain favor; next, instrumentals would have their turn.

When I arrived in Manhattan in 1949 love songs that were popular during the war began to lose favor. As lives returned to normal, people were in a gay mood, and witty, clever tunes like *Marezy Doats and Doezy Doats* (Mares eat oats and Does eat oats) became popular. I felt I could easily write novelty tunes and came up with *Be-Bah-Bo-Beep,* a song about a guy and a gal in a car with a horn that goes *Be-Bah-Bo-Beep,* the musical notes of which are G-B-D-B. Try them on your guitar or piano. This automobile horn greeting was very big back then, a personalized audio salutation.

The *Roberta Quinlan Show* was a popular program in the early days of television and she performed my song at the piano, beeping away on those G-B-D-B notes as she drove a Ford jalopy on a sound stage of NBC:

BE-BAH-BO-BEEP ©

Give me the straight open road and the
narrow old highway, singing a song as
rolling along I go.

I'll shout to the gang on the corner, hey,
who's going my way?
Pile in while I tell you 'bout someone I know.

(Chorus)

Have you seen that guy with a gal in a car
with a horn that goes Be-Bah-Bo-Beep?
That's the way they letcha know,
That they wanted to say hello.

Yes, I mean that guy with a gal in a car
with a horn that goes Be-Bah-Bo-Beep.
They were happy as could be,
When they tooted that melody.

It's a lively little flivver,
You can feel it shake and shiver,
So it's all that you can hardly do to t-t-talk.
You be careful what you call her,

It's a simple thing to stall her,
And I'll make the gang of you get out and walk.

I'll be that guy with a gal in a car
with a horn that goes Be-Bah-Bo-Beep,
If I ever get a car.
If I ever get a gal.

Regretfully, I was unable to get the song published. Perhaps I didn't try hard enough to find a home for it. I wrote a second novelty tune I felt would surely catch a publisher's eye:

I NEED A LITTLE OVEN ©

I Need a Little Oven,
Not too big or bright,
Just a Little Oven
To keep me warm at night.

I Need a Little Oven
And I don't know what to do,
Can I get a Little Oven from you?

(more)

I thought it was a clever song, with a funny twist. It was easy to sing, and had a strong melody, but I couldn't find a home for that one either. Perhaps publishers didn't think the public would understand the double entendre.

Television was in its infancy in the early '50s. The forerunner of the present day *Tonight Show*, for instance, was *Broadway Open House*, hosted by standup comedian Jerry Lester. Steve Allen's *Tonight in New York* was next, followed by the *Jack Paar Tonight Show*, and then the *Johnny Carson Tonight Show*.

As a Page Boy, I appeared on Jerry Lester's *Broadway Open House* with three of my brothers, twins Hap and Lucky (Clifton and Clifford) and another twin, George. One summer the three of them piled into my old Mercury convertible and drove from Chicago to New York to visit me. They slept in makeshift sleeping bags on the floor of my one-room Manhattan apartment off 55th and Lexington.

Prior to my conducting a special NBC tour for my brothers, we were in the NBC mezzanine lounge harmonizing to the song, *Once in Awhile,* when Jac Hein approached us. Jac was producer-director of *Broadway Open House.* An act had cancelled out of his show that evening and he asked if we'd like to appear in its place. We accepted, and it was fun, especially as we earned a big two hundred bucks which the boys used for gas money on the way home. We were so well received on the show that we were invited back a second night, even being offered a permanent spot on the show! Who knows? We might have gone on to become another Osmond Brothers team. It was an exciting offer, but reason prevailed and my brothers elected to finish their college educations.

One music publisher I hoped would be interested in my songs turned out to be a dud, at least from my standpoint. I was finally able to see him because his piano player didn't show up and I offered to fill in. The afternoon dragged on as I played songs written by every writer except myself. When it was my turn to demo my own songs, the phone rang and the publisher abruptly left the room for an appointment. On the way out the door he said, "Call my secretary. Maybe I can listen to your stuff next week."

Wrong! I didn't write "stuff." I could call it that, but not he. This wasn't a publisher I wanted to work with, no matter how eager I was to hook up with one. Perhaps I had an attitude problem and my pride got in my way. As I grew in the industry I learned to be more patient; publishing is a tough business and I had to get used to it.

When writing a song, lyricists forever struggle with trying to find the proper balance between words and music, often attempting to compensate for a weak melody line by contriving too cute or too clever a lyric. It's a judgment call. And so I kept at it, improving as I went along, and feeling good about my progress. When waltzes were in style I wrote

May I Have This Dream? I never found a buyer for it either, but I still like it. I think the words and the music are a good fit. Later, I published and recorded it myself:

MAY I HAVE THIS DREAM? ©

(Verse)

Though I close my eyes and meditate
And try to dream of you, dear.
I may fix a time, a place, and set a date,
But where are you, dear?

Maybe the right thing, polite thing to do
is less of a task, if only I'd ask you,

(Chorus)

May I Have This Dream?
Let me hold you tight.
May I Have This Dream?
Just this once tonight.

Though we're far apart
Your love still fills my heart.
Warm me with your smile,
Be with me for awhile, please

May I Have This Dream tonight?

Whatever the musical trend, I followed it, to no avail. The exercise was exhausting; I was going around in circles attempting to define my talents. I couldn't blame the publishers. The way I figured it if they could predict a winner, every song they published would be a hit. What they were able to do, however, was to take the easy road and imitate songs that were currently popular. It's simpler and less of a gamble to follow trends, providing one catches the wave at the crest and not the fall.

Early one evening after making the publisher rounds I stopped off at the Broadway Deli for a take-out pastrami sandwich and coffee. It was a cold and windy night. Store awnings were snapping in the air like firecrackers. Manhattan was drenched in rain, and people were scurrying for shelter in doorways and subway entrances as the lights of the city came on.

Soaked to the gills, I entered my apartment. On the bed was a small package postmarked *Indiana* which my trusty landlord had placed there. Sensing what might be in it I stared at the package for the longest time before mustering courage to open it. I had a funny feeling in my gut that something had gone wrong back home. Call it a sixth sense if you will. In the three months since graduation I had returned to Indiana twice to visit my fiancé, but detected no sign of a problem or even a concern.

I read only the opening words of her letter: "I hope you will understand, but . . ." Then I skipped to the part where she said goodbye. Inside the package were my fraternity pin and engagement ring. Three months into our engagement, she had met and married someone else. Alongside my writing desk was a metal wastebasket, and that's where I burned her letter and her picture. I don't pride myself for having done that. I'm not a bitter person, but if it best describes the hurt, anger, disgust, the total feeling of helplessness of that moment, then that's what I was. Where did things go wrong? With no clue as to what had happened, my mind grew numb reviewing the possible scenarios.

I'd been in some fairly heavy jungle rains, but they seemed mild compared to the storm slapping against my apartment windows. No matter, its fury seemed to match my own. Pulling up the collar of my jacket I left my room, walked down the hallway and out the front door. After allowing the rain to beat on my face awhile I descended the apartment steps and walked out into the night. If tears had dimmed my sight, my feet knew the way. I had walked this direction many times before: right to Lexington, right on 57th Street past Sutton Place, then up a few steps into a little granny park overlooking the East River.

It was a quiet place where one could go to gather his thoughts, reminisce, or plan for tomorrow. On a clear day you could see Brooklyn and Queens. Down below, a tug boat might pass by, laboring its heavy load through the cold water. Hell's Gate, that turbulent waterway leading out to Long Island, was off to the right. Big ships are known to have run aground there. Some were even swallowed up and devoured as they attempted to traverse this hungry whirlpool of fury. Welfare Island was just below and off to the left. How it got its name isn't clear. Some say the island housed a mental hospital or a shelter for the homeless, or a prison. No matter. All three were prisons of a sort.

Taking a seat on my favorite bench I stared numbly into the rainy night for what seemed an eternity. As if in a daze I rolled the engagement ring over and over in my hand, the emotion of the moment tearing at me. Turning my head upward I allowed the rain to beat harder on my face, anything to make the feeling go away.

How many times had I strolled up to this place? Where did three months go? All those lights out there, what was behind them? And all those cars on the bridge, who was in them? Where was everybody coming from? Where was everyone going? I asked the same questions of myself:

Who are you?

Where are you going?

Who cares?

I had work ahead of me. It would be a long while before I would allow myself to become romantically involved again. This time I vowed to keep that promise.

DON AND ME AT WORK

Our first published song

CHAPTER

Learning the Hard Way

No flame of desire can long continue to burn vigorously if its supply of suggestive fuel be cut off from it.

—Robert Collier

Bob Sour, co-writer of the pop standard *Body and Soul* was writer representative for the publishing company Broadcast Music, Inc. Of all the publishers I had visited, Bob saw something in my music, and as time went on he became my mentor. Whenever I finished a song I would bring it to him. Bob phoned me one afternoon to suggest I demonstrate some of my material for songwriter Ben Raleigh who had broken up with his writing partner, Bernie Wayne. Together this duo had collaborated on a hit song, *Laughing on the Outside, Crying on the Inside.*

Ben listened to one of my songs and then asked, "What are you doing, Stan, rhyming 'charming' with 'darling'? They don't rhyme, Stan." I didn't pass his test. Ben was looking for a finished writer, not a student. In the coming months I discovered many pop songs that did not adhere to traditional rhyming rules. The "pure rhyme" concept isn't a hard and fast rule, and many a hit song contains one or two accepted variations.

Renowned lyricist Roger Hammerstein II (*Oklahoma, King and I, Carousel, Sound of Music*), downplayed his role as lyricist while exalting composers. He said:

> *Music is a difficult subject. Words are easier to analyze. Everybody speaks and writes words. Few can write music. Its creation is a mystery. There are mathematical principles to guide its construction, but no mere knowledge of these can produce the emotional eloquence some music attains.*

Realizing my strength was in writing music, I was fortunate to hook up with an exceptional lyricist in Don Upton, an NBC Page with whom I collaborated on a regular basis. We worked out of NBC's Studio 9B, the "Fireside Room" from which President Franklin D. Roosevelt broadcast his famous fireside chats to the nation. It was an out-of-the-way studio, and it had the best-tuned piano in the building.

British performer Wendy Barrie taped her NBC television variety show out of 3B, a small, third floor studio. Wendy would always sign off her program with the admonition, "Be a good little bunny now." With that thought in mind Don and I wrote a song for her. Wendy invited me to perform it on her show and asked me to wear my uniform because she felt it was good public relations. I was presented with a classic Bulova wrist watch as an honorarium, a treasured memento of the early *Golden Days of Television* tucked away in my drawer of keepsakes.

FUNNY LITTLE BUNNY ©

With so much gloom in style,
Where did you get that smile?
A Funny Little Bunny like you.
You wrinkle up your nose and
trouble ups and goes,
A Funny Little Bunny are you.
You have a way of making me feel so carefree.
Dare me, and I betcha I touch the moon!

It's nice to have 'round,
I'm awful glad I found,
A Funny Little Bunny like you.

On my way to the Fireside Room I poked my head into the ninth floor observation booth overlooking NBC's immense Studio 8H where *Saturday Night Live* is now telecast. Shirley Burkhart, a tour guide and special friend, was conducting a tour. I stood at the rear of her group and listened to her spiel:

You are now looking into Studio 8H, the largest radio broadcasting studio in the world, built especially for Mr. Arturo Toscanini. At this moment, we are fortunate to be able to witness the maestro rehearsing the NBC Symphony Orchestra. The glass partition in front of us is double-paned and made of thick, one-way glass so as not to distract the maestro.

As I watched the performance I couldn't help but think how lucky I was to be able to watch one of Toscanini's rehearsals whenever I wished. I never knew what to expect. The maestro was a taskmaster who was known to throw his baton at a player when unhappy with his performance. I was never a witness to one of those tirades.

After waving to Shirley I left the observation booth and walked down the hall to the Fireside Room. Don was putting finishing touches on a new song:

IT'S NEW TO ME ©

Yesterday was Friday,
Friday wasn't my day.
Neither were the days and years before.
But today is Saturday,
My first it doesn't matter day,
And tonight's the night I'm waiting for.
Tonight I realize other loves are all passe',
But you, you're so, well, different,

That is, I mean to say,

(Chorus)

It's New To Me,
Darling what you do to me.
In your arms I'm hopelessly captured,
Charmed and enraptured by you.
It's New To Me,
Knowing someone's true to me,
Sharing every moment exciting,
Loving, delighting, we two.

That fascinating, captivating look
in your eyes,
Somehow it weaves a spell and dreams
begin to rise,
Thrilling dreams of willing schemes that
I've yet to know,
Don't let me go. I want to know,
So do to me,
Ev'rything that's new to me.
Let me know the joy of your kisses,
Darling, for this is so new.

I thought Don's lyric was one of his best and ventured the opinion that he could be another Larry Hart (*My Funny Valentine, Blue Room, Bewitched)*. I truly believed Don was that gifted. He later went on to excel in broadcasting at WIS-TV in Columbia, South Carolina where he met and married Miriam Stevenson, Miss Universe of 1954. Sadly, my friend died of an illness in 1978, much too young. Had his life not ended prematurely I believe he would have enjoyed a long and successful songwriting career. His way with words was clever, more stylized than mine. My task in writing music to his lyrics was always an interesting challenge.

Don wrote an exceptionally beautiful lyric to another of our songs, *So This Is Love*. His images are alternately simple, yet graphic in design. It is another of our songs that I would eventually record in my album of television themes:

SO THIS IS LOVE ©

So This Is Love.
My, you have a lovely place here.
Everything is hearts and lace here,
It's beautiful, beautiful.

So This Is Love.
Seems the sky is so much brighter.
Here on high my head seems lighter,
It's wonderful, wonderful.

Did you build this dream all by yourself?
And choose this heavenly view?
And tell me, do you live here all by yourself?
Why, it's big enough for two.

So This Is Love,
Nestled in a field of clover,
Awful glad you asked me over,
And if I may, I would like to stay.

When we weren't taking tours or writing songs, Don and I would venture to the rooftop of the RCA building for lunch. The air was invigorating up there and conversation flowed freely between us. We laughed, told stories, and often came up with new ideas during those times. Looking down at the city toward Broadway I surveyed the streets I treaded so often. I always had the feeling I was covering a lot of ground, but from this rooftop view I realized I had walked merely a few blocks in each direction.

Everyone wanted to help the underdog. Whenever I was planning to pitch a song to an NBC artist I would go to my locker room and put on my uniform. Perry Como's office was in the Radio City Music Hall building just across the street from NBC. I auditioned many songs for him, including *Christmas Eve in My Home Town,* but never made a sale. Many variables determine song selection, and I knew I was competing with some of the great songwriters of that era. An artist's time is valuable. As a neophyte writer I considered myself fortunate to be able to demonstrate songs to artists of Perry's stature.

In general, I wasn't much for socializing. Rarely would you find me at Cromwell's, a coffee shop and drug store on the main floor of NBC where Pages and Guides would gather. It seemed many wasted valuable time gabbing there instead of making business contacts. One day I dropped in at Cromwell's where my Guidette friend Shirley was having coffee with some of the Guest Relations staff. Shirley was my biggest fan, and knew practically all my music. That day she asked what I had in my portfolio. I told her it was a song she had heard before, *In the Harbor of My Heart.* She asked to see it.

IN THE HARBOR OF MY HEART ©

In the Harbor of My Heart,
That's where I want you to stay.
You'll always find a haven there,
A retreat from the storms of the day.

In the Harbor of My Heart
That's where I want you to be,
So I can mend the sails of your life
When they're torn by life's turbulent sea.

Now you say you're leaving
And I don't want you to go.
I have grown to love you
More than you'll ever know.

But if you must say farewell,
To sail again with the tide,
I'll be waiting for you,
Near a place set aside
In the Harbor of My Heart.

After reading the words she said, "This is good. You changed the ending. I like it. So what are you doing here?"

"You're right," I replied, "I'll see you later." With that I returned the song to my briefcase and headed for Tin Pan Alley. I placed the song with a good publisher but nothing ever happened with it. After a year it was returned to me.

In an industry where contacts are important you might think I would have welcomed any opportunity to establish a good connection, and you would be right. There was one special occasion where I rejected such an opportunity. It was at a dinner engagement with a lady friend at the Harriman Lodge, a rustic retreat in upstate New York. It was an interesting place overlooking the Hudson River, complete with a log-burning fireplace and an irresistible Steinway upright piano. I had no sooner finished playing a song or two when a young lady approached our table from across the room.

"The songs you played," she said, "I have never heard them before. They are good. Are they yours?"

I attempted to discourage a conversation, as I sensed where it was leading. "I'm looking for a writing partner," she continued. "If you will consider working with me I can get our songs to Mitch Miller at Columbia Records. His door is open to me any time I want. We can make a lot of money."

At any other time or place I might have been interested, but this was not one of them. "You know what, Miss," I said. "I believe your priorities are twisted. If your music is that good, money will follow, not the other way around. Thank you for the compliment, but I don't think we could work together."

CHAPTER 7

Getting Published

There's a way to do it better. Find it.

—Thomas Edison

Almost two years after my arrival in New York, and having written songs that never found a publishing home, Don and I wrote something that caught the ear of my mentor, Bob Sour: *Christmas Eve in My Home Town.* A yuletide song is probably the most difficult to get published, as there is so limited a selling season between Thanksgiving and Christmas. Yet, Bob saw something in ours that showed promise and said his company would publish it provided we were willing to make a certain lyric change. Hallelujah!

In all the excitement we didn't realize the revision would require more time and effort than it did to write the entire song. No matter, we were ready. After all, we had a prospective buyer in the wings! In the end the experience turned out to be a valuable lesson in composition, one we needed to learn.

There are many rhyming patterns. Ours fell into what is known as the A-A-B-A pattern. The key rhyme in the three A sections must match. Two did match, "mistletoe," in the first A, and "know" in the third A. However, the word "see" in the second A was not a rhyme. It was in this section that Bob wanted us to make the lyric change.

The internal rhymes within the B section were not a problem. They could stand alone, an accepted norm. We didn't touch this section.

The best way to explain how Don and I fixed the rhyme in the second "A" section is to show you the entire song as first written:

CHRISTMAS EVE IN MY HOME TOWN ©

"A" (The first eight, acceptable, measures)

Carols in the square,
Laughter everywhere,
Couples kissing under the mistletoe
I can't help reminiscing,
Knowing I'll be missing,
Christmas Eve in My Home Town.

"A" (The second eight, non-acceptable measure, because the word "see" doesn't rhyme with "mistletoe")

Winters come and go,
Holly leaves and snow,
Winters, never Christmases do I see,
There's so much to remember,
No wonder I remember,
Christmas Eve in My Home Town.

"B" (The third eight, acceptable measures, or "bridge" of the song)

I'd like to be there,
Trimming the tree there,
And there's a chance that I might.
I can hear singing,
Steeple bells ringing,
Noel and Silent Night.

"A" (The last eight, acceptable measures)

Wise men journeyed far,
Guided by a star,
But though I'm not a wise man, this I know,
Through dreams and just pretending
I'm there, and I'll be spending,
Christmas Eve in My Home Town.

We worked for days trying to find a matching "oh" rhyme for the second "A" section, but the answer never came. What we eventually decided to do was chuck the entire section and create a new thought on which to build the lyric. Once found, we would then concentrate on the rhyming problem.

Don and I now realized we had eight measures of a song with no point of view. How to fill that gap? We decided to zero in on the concept that no one could take away our recollections of the yuletide season. "Take away." Yes! That was the phrase that hit us, "Take away!"

Okay, now what word best implies taking something away? We went to our thesaurus and under "take away" we discovered a host of synonyms and came upon the juicy word, "erase." We wrote it down: "erase." Okay, erase what? What word rhymes with erase?

We went to our rhyming dictionary and found the very warm, meaningful word, "embrace." Now we had, "nothing can erase, the (something) I embrace." Okay. What "something" couldn't be erased, thoughts, experiences, memories? "Memories!" Yes! We wrote it down. "Nothing can erase, the 'memories' I embrace." Whatever memory it was, it needed to end in "oh" and we found the word, "snow."

Now, what to say about snow? What we had so far was, "Nothing can erase the memories I embrace of (something) in the snow." Okay, memories of what in the snow? Playing in the snow? Walking in the snow? Shoveling the snow? Somehow we came across the magical word, "footprints." That was it! "Nothing can erase the memories I embrace, the (something, something) footprints upon the snow." We added the word "familiar," and came up with "familiar footprints" and liked the alliteration as well.

Putting together the entire thought, the end result was:

Nothing can erase
The mem'ries I embrace,
Those familiar footprints upon the snow.
There's so much to remember,
No wonder I remember
Christmas Eve in My Home Town.

We finally had our three rhymes: "mistletoe," "snow," and "know." The thoughts behind the rhymes worked for us. The lyrics fell easily off the tongue and peaked with the music where appropriate. Everything fit. That was the guiding word. If something did not "fit," it had to be fixed, whatever it was.

Joyously, almost hysterically, Don and I tucked the manuscript under our arms and waltzed across town to present our treasure to Bob Sour. He liked it. That day in 1951 we assigned publishing rights to Mr. Sour's company, Broadcast Music, Inc.

It has always been a mystery to me how some truly wonderful songs never get heard or recorded, while others seemed to find favor early on and become an immediate success. Over the years *Christmas Eve in My Home Town* has taken on a life of its own. The publishing rights changed hands three times before my company, Big Island Music, Inc. assumed ownership.

At last count there were seventeen commercial recordings, including those by Kate Smith, Bobby Vinton, Jim Nabors, Eddie Fisher, The Living Strings, The Living Voices, Masters of Harmony and notable barbershop ensembles. The First Infantry Band in Korea has recorded a marching band version, as has the United States Army Field Band, *The Army Ambassadors of Music.* Symphonic orchestras and college groups, have added their renditions, notably Anthony Bisbano's swing arrangement for songstress Addi McDaniel.

Performance licenses are issued regularly to non-profit schools and charitable organizations. In 2012, *The Victory Belles* vocal and dance troupe performed the song at The National World War II Museum in New Orleans.

Over the years, thanks to former record producer Jenny Hudson, *Readers Digest* included *Christmas Eve in My Home Town* in seven of its holiday CD packages. Thomas Kincaid included the song in his set of Christmas favorites. Music publisher Frank Hackinson and Dave Olsen, then of Warner-Chappell Music, remain champions of the song.

But from the beginning it was our mentor, writer-publisher Bob Sour, who saw something in *Christmas Eve in My Home Town* that convinced him to take a chance on our song. Today it is offered in many forms on the Internet and I-phones and is listed in Ron Clancy's prestigious and highly acclaimed two-volume book and CD set, "*Best Loved Christmas Carols.*"

Plays His Song

Sgt. Stan Zabka, young Chicago composer, playing his song, "Christmas Eve in My Home Town," for army buddies as they departed on navy transport from New York for service in Europe.

The Troop Ship, U.S.N.S. General R. E. Callan (T-AP139)

Korea Calls

For all your days prepare, and meet them ever alike. When you are the anvil, bear. When you are the hammer, strike.

—Edward Markham

The good news of *Christmas Eve* finding a publishing home was overshadowed by the darkness of world events. In the Pacific, America was in the midst of the Korean War, while across the Atlantic our country's Cold War with Russia showed no signs of being resolved. On a visit home to Chicago I found the city ringed with missile silos and anti-aircraft batteries set up along Lake Michigan's North Shore and in Soldiers Field.

As mentioned earlier, most of our armed forces had been disbanded after World War II, and as a consequence the defense capability of the United States had been thrust into serious jeopardy. In that context, the likelihood that non-married veterans would be recalled to military service was a distinct possibility. This fact was confirmed when I returned to New York.

My tour group had arrived at an observation window just as NBC announcer Ken Banghart was winding down his hourly newscast.

Switching on the hall speaker we listened as Ken completed a news story:

> *... in what may yet prove to be one of the bloodiest wars in history. Since the North Korean troops invaded South Korea on June 25th, sixteen UN countries have sent troops to help the South Koreans. Forty one countries have sent military equipment or food and other supplies. With China's entry into the war on the side of North Korea, and the cold war escalating with Russia, there is speculation that, since US forces were scaled back after World War II, single veterans of that conflict may, of necessity, be called back into military service. In Europe itself, meanwhile ...*

With that, the air went silent as someone in my tour group reached up and turned off the wall speaker. In an attitude of obvious disgust he blurted out, "I knew we were going to have trouble with those damn Russians!"

Another tourist concurred. "Patton was right," he said. "We should've gone right through Moscow when we had a chance!"

This was not idle chatter. Americans were coming to terms with the real possibility of being involved in another two-ocean war. Territorial ambitions, nuclear weapons and space exploration were core issues of our country's dispute with Russia. Diplomatically there seemed to be no exit strategy. These were not good times.

Talk around the building concerned the little-known existence of NBC's own Army Reserve Unit. Apparently the United States had no psychological warfare units in place when World War II broke out, as had the Japanese and Germans. To correct that imbalance, NBC's President General David Sarnoff established the *301st Broadcast and Leaflet Group*. Films on atomic weaponry and psychological warfare techniques were shown at bi-monthly meetings held in one of NBC's broadcast studios. I attended one such meeting to check it out.

The 301st was made up of two media groups, NBC and the *New York Daily News*. NBC personnel provided the broadcast arm to disseminate information and propaganda via mobile units. The print division was manned by *Daily News* personnel and was charged with providing leaflets to be dropped from aircraft or otherwise distributed by hand through towns and villages.

Intellectually, while the combined IQ of the 301st was extremely high, much higher than that required for Officer Candidate School, the fact remained that less than half the group had seen prior military service. The rest were unfamiliar with command authority of any kind, nor were they accustomed to taking or issuing orders. No question about it, were this unit to be activated it would be one tough cookie to manage. Still, I reasoned that if I was to be called back into military service I might as well remain in broadcasting, and decided to join NBC's *301st Broadcasting and Leaflet Group.*

I was offered the rank of Staff Sergeant, two stripes below the top enlisted rank of Master Sergeant. I figured it was a fair offer since I had been discharged a Corporal from World War II. Being a college graduate didn't matter either, as practically everyone in the 301st had a degree of one sort or another.

It was near closing time when I entered the Army Recruiting Center on Wall Street. The master sergeant on duty must have had a heavy date lined up as he kept looking at his wrist watch. I figured he must've served in every war since Noah, as hash marks denoting length of time in service ran from the cuff of his left sleeve to halfway up his arm. On his chest were more ribbons and decorations than a Christmas tree, including two Purple Hearts. The dialogue between us that late afternoon was right out of a movie script. To the best of my recollection here's how the scene played out:

"This NBC group you're joining is General Sarnoff's baby, you know. We didn't have a unit like this during World War II. He formed this one so we would be ready."

"That's what they tell me."

"Sarnoff owns NBC."

"Actually, he owns RCA. RCA owns NBC."

"Yeah, well that's what I mean. Damn, it's Friday, near closing time. Couldn't you have gotten here sooner? I got a hot date."

"I'll bet."

"Beg your pardon?"

"I was just saying, I wonder where you met?"

"Blind date, actually."

"Gorgeous, no doubt."

"A living doll. Big bazooms. Plus, she digs these stripes and all these ribbons. Babes are crazy for glitter, you know? You got a babe?"

"I used to. You must have women crawling all over you, Sarge."

"I do okay. It's tough operating in this town, lots of competition from the Wall Street honchos. What can I say?"

"With your top rank and good looks you have everything going for you. You are probably independently wealthy, too."

"I wish I was. By the way, this NBC unit you are joining, it's scheduled to go to Europe, you know. The San Francisco outfit is going to Korea."

"How do you know that?"

"It's my job to know. That's why they pay me the big bucks. You would understand if you had been around the block a few times like I have."

"I'm sure."

"You know what, you're good. Real good. The Army needs sharp cookies like you and me. What rank did they put you down for in this outfit?

"Staff Sergeant, I think. I was discharged a Corporal.

"Why don't we take you up to five stripes? Make you a Sergeant First Class, one grade below me?"

"Why not?"

"Dust off your old uniform, Sarge. You'll be needing it soon."

As it turned out, he was right. The San Francisco psychological warfare unit did ship out to Korea. A month or so later sixty members of NBC's 301st Broadcast and Leaflet Group scheduled for European duty were activated and sent to Ft. Riley, Kansas for indoctrination and training. This broadcast group was joined by fifty-two journalists from the *New York Daily News,* including its owner and editor, Lt. James Patterson.

As civilians, many of us in the 301st had known each other from work or from group meetings. Still others of us had palled around New York, gone skiing, or otherwise double-dated. Now, practically overnight, we found ourselves in uniforms with military ranks and titles. Some of us were privates, some were corporals or sergeants, and some were officers. While some were giving orders, all of us were taking them in one fashion or the other.

Non-veterans found it difficult to make the switch from civilian to military life. Command authority or any resemblance of respect for rank was almost a joke, to say the least. It was pathetic. No one wanted to obey anyone. If ever there was an eclectic bunch of malcontents not primed for overseas duty it was the 301st Broadcast and Leaflet Group. This, then, was the crack outfit that boarded the troopship USS Callan in mid-1951 bound for Europe and The Cold War with Russia.

It was also a time when my first song had been published. The event did not go unheralded by my mentor and publisher, Bob Sour. As the 301st prepared to embark from New York Harbor he came aboard ship and presented me with printed sheet music of *Christmas Eve in My Home Town.* Singing idol Johnny Desmond's picture was on the cover, as he was scheduled to record the song. Bob also presented me with a 78rpm recording by country singer Roy Stevens. In the next instant an upright piano was rolled into the ship's lounge and Bob had reporters snapping pictures as I played the song. I still have a copy of the sheet music signed by my buddies. Many signatures are faded now, but I can still read most of the names and remember many of those who signed it.

As the good ship USS Callan crossed the Atlantic we staged some fun music and variety shows on board. All prospective thespians and would-be entertainers met daily in the nurses' lounge to write and rehearse. This was a welcome change from having to remain in the enlisted men's section of the ship. In my portfolio was a song Don and I had written, a catchy tune about nurses that seemed appropriate for one of the variety shows. I performed it on stage with one of them.

MERCY, NURSEY ©

Oh, they say that you're an angel of mercy.
(She) *Angel of Mercy?*
(Me) *Uh huh. Angel of Mercy.*
But you're more than any angel of mercy,
'Cause MERCY, NURSEY, you're an angel to me.

And they say that you're a Florence Nightingale.
(She) *Nightingale?*
(Me) *Uh huh, Nightingale.*
But you're more than any Florence Nightingale,
'Cause MERCY, NURSEY, you're an angel to me.

Oh my, ain't I done everything I should?
I wanta please ya.
Dearie, when you're near me, you make me feel
so good, I wanta squeeze ya.

You're a pretty little lady dressed in white.
(She) *Cute and bright?*
(Me) *Uh huh. Dressed in white.*
I wish you'd add a veil and kneel in candlelight,

And MERCY NURSEY for better or worsey,
Nursey, for better or worsey,
Nursey, for better or worsey, marry me.

After a few days our group disembarked at the German port of Bremerhaven. From there we motored to the town of Mannheim where we were assigned barracks that had once housed German troops. These were not tents or Quonset Huts; these were strong units, solidly built of concrete and brick, with high bushes and trees surrounding the compound. No question, its previous occupants enjoyed top of the line living quarters.

As weeks and then months dragged by, improved relations with the USA caused Russia to retreat from its hard line strategy. As a result, there was no longer any reason for our group being in Europe. To keep us busy we were assigned menial tasks, taught foreign languages, and were otherwise compelled to participate in endless marches through the Black Forest. It was a sad time. Low morale in the 301st was literally crippling the group. To compound the issue, many families back home, weary of the military in the first place and struggling financially to stay afloat, were in danger of disintegrating.

My own First Sergeant, a former NBC executive who had relinquished a top sales spot to join the 301st, actually went berserk. As if needing some sort of protection he acquired a Doberman as a companion. On one windy, rainy day while watching his men dig mock graves his mind snapped. Seeing his life waste away in this fashion apparently was too much for this WWII veteran. When he and his dog returned to his billets they literally tore the room to shreds. The Army put him in rehab for awhile and then sent him home. I lost track of him after that.

As time wore on, many in the 301st sought transfers to any European army unit that had an opening. One Master Sergeant managed a lateral transfer to Army Headquarters in Heidelberg, the first of six personnel permitted to leave the group. From that vantage point whenever an opening occurred in our sector, and he felt someone in the 301st could fill the slot, he would notify that person and cut transfer orders.

My job with the 301st was Headquarters Supply Sergeant. I was charged with counting bed sheets and foot lockers and otherwise keeping tabs on the group's inventory of equipment and supplies. To avoid going batty myself I attempted to write new songs and correspond with Don in New York, but never seemed to muster sufficient desire or energy to concentrate. My life was in limbo with no clear direction or purpose and I was powerless to do anything about it.

One afternoon I was tuned into the American Forces Network (AFN) and heard Master Sergeant Mel Riddle winding up his newscast. AFN headquarters was located in a castle in the small village of Hoechst, just south of Frankfurt. The network was created in England by General Eisenhower in 1943 to help boost troop morale by disseminating news and music from home. With its twelve stations spread across Europe and 150,000 watts of power, AFN reached more listeners than the Voice of America and Radio Free Europe combined. The Voice of America is still active, but Radio Free Europe (also known as Radio Liberty) is not. It was disbanded after the Cold War. Some believe it still exists in the Czech Republic, but only underground.

Following Sergeant Riddle's newscast, "The Baron of Bounce," Ken Dunnagan, was on the air at AFN, playing his brand of swing and jazz music. A surge of energy suddenly coursed through my veins. In my desk drawer was the 78 RPM recording of my Christmas song. Without hesitation I picked it up, placed it next to me in my jeep, and was on my way to AFN to see if I could get it played. I arrived in less than an hour, weaving my jeep through the winding, cobblestone streets of Hoechst until I arrived at the Von Bruening Castle. Over the entranceway of this imposing edifice was a rainbow-shaped sign that read:

YOU ARE ENTERING THE HEADQUARTERS OF THE AMERICAN FORCES NETWORK, EUROPE

From that moment on, the direction of my military life took a dramatic turn, and the opportunity to continue my songwriting aspirations received a major, unpredictable boost.

AMERICAN FORCES NETWORK HEADQUARTERS, EUROPE

CHAPTER 9

Opportunity Knocks at AFN

I have always believed that anybody with a little guts and the desire to apply himself can make it, can make anything he wants to make of himself.

—Willie Shoemaker

Driving through the entranceway I paused to survey the manicured grounds, the surrounding moat, and the Neckar River where a constant stream of boats made their way. This was no ordinary broadcast studio, this was a castle, and a famous one at that, where Napoleon is said to have stayed. I wondered how it functioned, where the studios and various departments were located, and if its staff of broadcasters were housed on the premises.

My first stop was the record library, which the sergeant in charge told me was the largest in the world. The Enlisted Men's Lounge across the courtyard had been the stables, while the broadcast studios, news room, and executive offices were upstairs in what had once been family living quarters. The sergeant went on to say that AFN's enlisted personnel were billeted in the castle tower, while AFN's four officers maintained separate housing in town. The "Mess Hall" was located in a private residence near the castle.

No question about it, I thought, *reporting for duty here must be a joy!* As for getting my Christmas record played, the librarian said it would not be possible. AFN was a government network and all programming had to be cleared through the Armed Forces Radio and Television Service (AFRTS) in Los Angeles. *So much for that effort,* I thought. *It was a good try.*

I left the record library and walked across the courtyard to the enlisted men's lounge for a cup of coffee. Reading a magazine at the bar was Master Sergeant Mel Riddle, the announcer I had heard delivering the news, and we struck up a conversation. Mel mentioned that he also was Military News Chief of the network, but that he was leaving AFN to re-enter politics in California. When he inquired as to what sort of work I was engaged in back home I told him I was on the guest relations staff of NBC in New York taking people on tour of its studios. I also mentioned that I had apprenticed on many of the network's news and special events programs, which prompted him to ask questions about stateside broadcasting and what changes were taking place there.

Mel then said he had an idea. Asking if I would mind waiting a few minutes he left the lounge. In the brief discussion on his return he told me AFN was looking for someone with my rank and experience to take his place as News Chief and asked if I would like the job. The question struck me like a lightning bolt. At first I didn't believe he was serious, but before I knew it I was being escorted upstairs to talk to AFN's program director and sports announcer, Lt. Tom Decker. AFN's Commanding Officer Colonel Philip Johnson soon joined the conversation. The colonel was easy to converse with, an unassuming person with the manner and bearing of a southern gentleman you read about in history books. Later on I learned he was a highly decorated infantry officer and that among his many decorations was the French *Crois de Guerre* for valor in combat.

In the interview that followed I was asked about my radio experience at college. I explained that I had received a broadcast scholarship as director of our campus station and that my degree was in communications and music. As for my job with NBC, I made it clear that while I had been hired as a Page Boy and worked as an apprentice on some of its shows, including *The Big Show*, my principle assignment was taking people on tour of its studios.

The discussion then turned to my present outfit in Mannheim, the 301st Broadcasting and Leaflet Group, why it was activated in the first place, what its current mission was, and whether I was wedded to my job as supply sergeant. After further discussion Colonel Johnson then said that unless I wanted to continue counting bed sheets and foot lockers, AFN would like to offer me Mel's job. He then added that AFN could use some help in the music area as well.

What a day! I had come to AFN to get a record played and now I was being offered the top spot as Military News Chief of the American Forces Network, Europe. The discussion didn't end there. "I'm going to be meeting with Eddie Fisher this week," the colonel added, "Mel tells me you showed some songs to him back home. He's Private First Class Eddie Fisher now, you know, over here to entertain our troops. Perhaps together we can convince him to record your Christmas song. We need some excitement around here."

As the colonel left the room he asked for a copy of the recording "to play for my wife, Ginnie," he said. "And by the way," he continued, "I'm heading to Heidelberg on some business. Why don't you follow me in your jeep and we'll cut your transfer papers while I'm at headquarters doing other business?"

It wasn't much later that the Army newspaper *Stars and Stripes* carried an article saying I was the last person allowed to leave the 301st Broadcast and Leaflet Group.

At the castle I was offered a room in the tower with commanding views of the village on one side and the Neckar River on the other. I had read about castles in story books, *King Arthur and The Knights of the Round Table,* and more, but I never imagined I would be living in one. And, not missing a beat, I was back in broadcasting, writing and preparing news for a dozen AFN stations across Europe. Later on I would be given my own weekly music program as well.

PREPARING THE EVENING NEWS

Discussing a story with George Homcy

Ten minutes to air time

In no time my musical ambitions were fired up, and in my off hours I collaborated long distance with my friend and colleague, Don Upton. We discussed new song ideas by audio tape. Since we had worked together very well in the past it was easy for me to write music to his words, even from a distance. At home we had been working on one of his new songs, *Don't Smile*. When I completed the music I sent him a copy. I believe it was one of his most expressive lyrics:

PREMIERE OF A SONG

Introducing a new song each week over AFN

DON'T SMILE ©

Don't Smile,
Unless you want the stars to hide.
Every star seems dim beside your lovely smile.

Don't Laugh,
Unless you'd have the stream grow still.
Rippling waters flow until they hear your laughter.

I'm not the only one to thrill at your eyes as they glisten.
For you, both the moon and sun would stop, and look, and listen.

Don't Speak,
The universe would heed your call.
Nature on its knees would fall,
As I do now.

Another recording star, Corporal Vic Damone, was soldiering in Europe along with PFC Eddie Fisher. Sinatra claimed he had the best pipes in the business. Reportedly Vic wasn't happy with the Army, believing Eddie was being accorded more "star" status than he. Vic was stationed in Nuremberg, about a hundred miles north of Munich. I visited him there a few times hoping I might convince him to record *Christmas Eve in My Home Town* for AFN. One evening after dinner and a movie I gave it the old college try one more time, but not having received a definitive answer from Damone, I pursued the matter no further.

Fortunately, Eddie Fisher did agree to record the song. In spite of a hefty entertainment schedule, and principally through Colonel Johnson's personal effort, a recording date was set for mid-December at the Eagle Club in Wiesbaden. This was welcome news, as Christmas 1952 was fast approaching. To back Eddie I hired Lutz Dietmar and his band, a Glenn Miller-type, German aggregation with its own entertainment and travel schedule to consider. More than once it appeared the recording date would be postponed. Band parts had to be copied and there were some printing errors that needed correcting. Still, plans came together in surprisingly smooth military fashion. And then something happened over which I had neither knowledge nor control.

Lieutenant Tom Decker called me into his office to say that Fisher had backed out. He said Eddie was miffed because whenever he appeared at an AFN station one of our disc jockeys would jam a copy of my Christmas song into his hand. I explained to Tom that this wasn't my intention. All I had hoped our disc jockeys would do was to see if artists in their respective locales would perform the song. I never mentioned Eddie's upcoming recording date to anyone, mainly because Colonel Johnson requested it remain a surprise.

This was a disappointing turn of events and I was one unhappy camper. Tom advised me to sleep on it overnight and said he would get back to me as soon as he had a chance to speak with Eddie again. For the longest time I gazed out one window of my room, and then the next. Restless, I left the tower. Strolling along the castle wall I watched the night lights coming on in the village beyond. The scenario reminded me of a similar trek I made to the East River in Manhattan the year before. Now I found myself dealing with similar emotions of disappointment, frustration, even despair.

When morning came, I crossed the moat to the enlisted men's lounge for a cup of coffee and met with Lieutenant Decker. Tom said the recording project was back on track. He was as pleased as I. Apparently the trouble centered on an AFN Bremerhaven sergeant who was traveling with Fisher. Hoping for assistance when he returned to civilian life, this sergeant was doing all of Fisher's valet chores, advising him on what appearances to make, which projects to take on. Basically, he was serving as his personal manager, often creating problems that didn't exist. Furthermore, he was traveling without a pass. As for Eddie's complaint about the AFN DJs, it turns out the subject had been blown out of proportion and was no longer an issue.

Fisher was staying at the Frankfurterhof Hotel and wanted me to join him there to coach him on the song. Tom sent one of our sergeants, Jim O'Gorman, to accompany me and to keep an eye on the Bremerhaven sergeant. If he caused any problem, Jim was instructed to report him for leaving his post without authorization.

Eddie rehearsed the song with me a few times while running an electric razor across his face. He seemed to be in a good mood, actually looking forward to being back in a recording studio. I found him to be a quick learner and had the feeling he had been rehearsing the song on his own. Following a light breakfast at the Frankfurterhof we piled into a staff car and drove to the Eagle Club in Wiesbaden.

Eddie first greeted Colonel Johnson, the person chiefly responsible for Eddie being there. A scattering of European military brass and their ladies were present, all invited guests of the colonel. After Eddie was introduced to Lutz Dietmar and the band, Lutz asked if I would like to lead his orchestra. This was a most gracious gesture on his part, as I was sure he had looked forward to conducting the famous singer himself. Delighted for the opportunity, I accepted. We recorded the song twice, listened to playbacks of both, and wrapped the session. Before leaving the Eagle Club Eddie asked if he might tape a message to a friend in the U.S. Defense Department and others in the nation's capitol:

> *Hello Major, and hello to everyone in the listening audience. This is your PFC again. We are here in Wiesbaden, Germany, recording a song, a very beautiful Christmas song which was written by a GI over here, a very dear friend of mine, Sergeant First Class, Stan Zabka. I knew him when he was working at a radio station, and I would like to dedicate this song to our Armed Forces and to all the folks back home. We have recorded this through the facilities of the American Forces Network. Let's listen to the song, shall we? Here it is, Stan Zabka's* Christmas Eve in My Home Town.

To sample Eddie's recording go to www.zabka.com

Adding to the day's special event, a fresh blanket of snow covered the castle grounds and the village of Hoescht with its quaint houses and shops adorned with colorful Christmas lights. Villagers gathered at the Red Ox Inn to meet "PFC Eddie," as they called him, and to hear a recording of his new Christmas song. The evening was special for another reason. A local resident asked Eddie if he would sing Franz Gruber's *Silent Night,* to which he obliged, singing it a cappella. Part way into the song the men of the village set aside their steins of beer and joined him in the most beautiful harmony imaginable. It was a moment to remember. A message to Don in New York brought him up to date:

> *Dear Don,*
> *We celebrated the recording of our song at the Red Ox Inn near the castle. It was a wonderful event, spontaneous, relaxed. Colonel Johnson had arranged the entire affair. He and Eddie have become good friends. The colonel loves music, claiming it is what brought us together in the first place. I wish you could have been here with us. This was your evening as well as mine. At one point I talked with Milt Blackstone, Fisher's manager, who came over for*

the occasion. He said I should contact him when I returned home, that maybe RCA would do a commercial recording with Eddie and Hugo Winterhalter's Orchestra and Chorus. I assured him that I would certainly take him up on his offer.
Best, Stan

The hustle and bustle of the Yuletide season had no sooner quieted down when the villagers and castle personnel began gearing up for the New Year. Europeans know how to have fun, and they were ready to party. Nursing a beer in the enlisted men's lounge I wondered what the future might hold for me. I was twenty-nine years old, had soldiered in the Pacific, worked in Hollywood, finished college, traveled to New York, became a published songwriter, re-entered the army with an NBC unit, and transferred to AFN as its military news chief. In another year or more I would be a civilian again. Of one thing I was certain: having enjoyed some success in music I definitely would continue that pursuit. What I didn't relish was the likelihood of putting on another uniform and returning to NBC as a Page Boy.

Sipping my last drop of beer I realized that I had some career-planning to do, and was reminded of the story of three young boys who were tracking their footsteps in the snow. They were having a contest to see which could walk the straightest line. For two of the boys their lines were not straight, although they said they had not taken their eyes off the ground. The line for the third boy hardly varied, and was straight as an arrow. How he accomplished it, he said, was by fixing his eye on a distant object, not looking down, but straight ahead, until he had reached his goal.

I would think about that tomorrow. At the moment, I was not in the mood. New Years was ahead. It was celebration time, time to get away. Thumbing through a stack of travel brochures I searched for a destination, somewhere I had never been before, preferably a place where I could do some serious skiing. Thumbing through a winter issue of *Esquire* magazine I found just what I was looking for, the captivating, snow-clad mountains of Switzerland!

CHAPTER 10

The Switzerland Story

Don't forget until too late that the business of life is not business, but living.
—Forbes

I had always wanted to visit the country famous for its coo-coo clocks and wrist watches. Scanning the *Esquire* pages further, I found pictures of a charming, secluded village high in the Swiss Mountains, the colorful village of St. Moritz. Travel brochures described it as the winter retreat of social high-flyers, minor European royalty, and the international jet set. Being in the army I didn't quite fit that description, but no matter. St. Moritz seemed the ideal place to usher in the New Year.

With two three-day passes in my possession I packed some civilian duds and boarded a train for Zurich. Once there I transferred to a shuttle tram for a winding trip through colorful little villages until we reached the mountain top where St. Moritz was located. With skiers negotiating the slopes around us we passed the village of Davos, where down-hill bobsledding competition drew excited crowds during the 1948 Winter Olympics.

Arriving in St. Moritz I found it to be just as I had seen in the brochures: narrow streets and icicle-laden structures awash with newly fallen snow, clanging bells on horse-drawn sleighs, and beyond the town square, inviting ski trails. The first place I visited was the American Express office to get some additional francs, but once there I learned I had made a big mistake. Before leaving Frankfurt I had opened an American Express checking account instead of obtaining travelers checks. Now, except for a few hundred francs in my wallet, I literally had no funds, and it was New Year's weekend. I was told I would have to wait until the following Monday to verify my American Express account with Frankfurt.

"Where will you be staying in St. Moritz?" I was asked. When I replied that I had no hotel reservations, the American Express lady said, "Oh, Sergeant, there are no openings anywhere in the village. People make reservations for St. Moritz years in advance. What are you going to do?"

Well, that was nice. I was without money and had no place to stay. Apparently the American Express lady felt I was a good risk, or because I was still in my army uniform. In any event, she was kind enough to advance me a few hundred francs and suggested I seek help at the American Embassy in town. She also advised that I visit the Courverein, a haven for wayward travelers such as myself.

"If these two places can't help you, Sergeant," she said, "you might just go door to door in the village to see if anyone has an empty room." I followed all her suggestions, with no luck. Even being in uniform was of no advantage. There wasn't an available bed in town.

Strolling from place to place I wandered into the most elegant establishment I had ever seen, the ultra-luxurious Palace Hotel. Across its spacious lobby was a young lady enjoying a view of the distant mountains from one of the hotel's glass-enclosed observation areas. Striking up a conversation I learned that she was the daughter of an ambassador of some country or other and that she and her family were staying at the Palace for the winter. I soon woke up to the fact that I hadn't walked into a Holiday Inn or South Chicago YMCA. I couldn't have stayed at the Palace even if there were a vacancy. Sheepishly, I excused myself and exited the hotel.

The evening air was biting. Walking around the corner and down the street from the Palace I came upon a nondescript yet charming little hotel, the Belvedere. Luck was with me. As I entered the lobby a young couple was just checking out. I was offered their room, at least for the night, with the possibility of retaining the room for the remainder of my stay. In the next hour I changed out of my uniform, showered, slipped into some civvies, and headed for the cocktail lounge with its baby grand piano. No sooner had I ordered a drink, lit my pipe, and began rambling over the keys when an elegant, middle aged lady approached. Introducing herself as Madame Fournier, she was quick to point out that her husband was Pierre Fournier, and that they were staying at the Belvedere.

Pierre Fournier! From my music studies I recalled that, next to Pablo Casals, he was the world's foremost cellist. Without hesitation, Madame Fournier then let it be known that she had previously been married to noted composer-conductor, Serge Koussevitzky. *What next*? I thought. Having made the acquaintance of an ambassador's daughter, I now found myself mixing with music royalty! Without hesitation I switched from playing cocktail music to playing the classics, *Claire de Lune,* to be specific. Madame Fournier would have none of it and stopped me by saying, "Oh no, no, please play your American music. It's so charming. And you must meet my husband."

Turning to his table, she called out, "Pierre, darling, please come. You must meet my new friend." Before I knew it, Madame Fournier was assuming the role of matchmaker. "Do you have a lady friend here in St. Moritz?" she asked. "You must find one and then we can all dine together. And you must bring her to watch Pierre rehearse on his 'silent cello'." I didn't know there was such a thing as a "silent cello." She then went on to explain that it was an instrument with no sound box, only a rib with frets and strings. "The hotel provides Pierre with a small room where he can be alone and practice his fingering," she said.

The maestro appeared a bit agitated. "Oh darling," he said, "he doesn't want to watch me practice."

"Oh, hush, love" she replied. "Of course he does, and he will bring a lady friend, won't you, Stanley?"

I did. I caught her eye on the porch of one of the ski lodges, and when I tossed an orange to her she thought it was a clever (American) way to say hello. She was from Herzoghenbuchsee, a tiny Swiss village near Bern. It was a classic instance of city boy meets country girl, and we had fun times with the Fourniers. She was fond of music, and when the moment presented itself we enjoyed watching the maestro practice on his silent cello. The four of us especially enjoyed riding through the village and surrounding hills in an open horse-drawn sleigh. At Madame Fournier's insistence, when New Years rolled around we celebrated it together.

We stayed in touch after I returned to AFN. I had a weekly radio program called *Premier of a Song* where I would introduce one of my compositions each week, and she listened to my programs in Switzerland. Sometimes she would visit me at the castle, and one weekend we drove to Heidelberg to attend a concert at the university. Her favorite classical pianist was Romanian artist Dinu Lipatti, and she introduced me to his recordings.

When I returned to civilian life my Swiss Miss joined me in London where I was recording some music. On another occasion we rendezvoused on the Italian Riviera and then motored to the tiny city of Carrara where Michelangelo carved his finest marble. From there we drove to Florence and visited the Uffizi Art Gallery where his magnificent statue of *David* is located.

Everyone adored her, including brother Hap who visited her in Switzerland while he was stationed in Verdun, France. It was through this wonderful person that I learned the true meaning of love. No promises, no fraternity pins, no engagement rings, just love.

When she turned twenty-one her father told her she could have anything she wanted for her birthday and she chose to visit me in New York. We toured all the sights, including NBC where I was working. We attended some concerts, and went shopping for a new wardrobe, American style. Once or twice during her visit I thought of asking her to marry me. However, given my past, unsuccessful romantic trysts I did not feel competent in making so strong a commitment. Before she returned to Switzerland I actually did propose marriage, but when she asked me what I had said I backed off, claiming I was just "thinking out loud."

Eventually she married a man from the Italian part of Switzerland. They had one child, a daughter. She phoned me from New York one day to tell me her mother had passed away and asked her to call and tell me goodbye.

I had a second but brief encounter with one other young lady before leaving St. Moritz. The interlude took place while ice skating leisurely at a mountaintop resort. I was wearing a snazzy maroon jacket and smoking my trusty pipe when a girl caught my eye that was performing an amazing series of twists and turns and jumps, the likes of which I had never seen. She was far superior to any skater on the rink, male or female. *Somehow,* I thought, *I've got to meet this girl*! Suddenly, with one grand gesture she concluded her routine with a fancy turn and double leap, stopping directly in front of me. Seizing the moment I introduced myself and offered the observation that while she skated beautifully I never saw her smile, even when she was executing the simplest maneuvers. This was true. She seemed so serious.

To add credence to my comment I told her that back in the States I had worked with the famous Norwegian ice skater, Sonja Henie. I lied. Furthermore, I mentioned that Miss Henie had confided that the secret of her success both in competition and in the movies was her ready smile.

It would have been wiser of me had I held my tongue, as this young lady's polite reply was most embarrassing: "You are absolutely right," she said. "Presently, I am amateur figure skating champion of the world. Right now I am practicing for the Olympics. And yes, I am very serious when I am concentrating."

You may have heard of this young lady, Tenley Albright, of Massachusetts. After practicing at St. Moritz she went on to win the 1952 Silver Medal, the 1953–1955 World Championship, the 1955 North American Championship, and the 1952–1956 National Championship. At the 1956 Winter Olympics in Italy, she became the first American female skater to win an Olympic Gold Medal!

Need I say more?

Singers, Barbara Hammond and Stan

CHAPTER 11

On the Road Again

I've never been poor, only broke. Being poor is a frame of mind. Being broke is only temporary. I can fix that.

—Mike Todd

Midway into 1953 my tour of duty in Europe was completed. In those days employers were required to re-hire returning veterans. I was hopeful NBC would offer me something other than my former Page Boy job, perhaps something in the network's vast news division where I could utilize my broadcasting experience with AFN. My timing wasn't good. I was told the company was in the midst of an economic cutback, and rather than firing its present employees it was asking them to take leaves of absence without pay. NBC was not dodging the issue; that's just the way it was. When I declined the Page Boy offer, the company promised to contact me when the job picture improved and a suitable position opened up.

Don, meanwhile, had accepted an announcing job with radio station WLVA in Lynchburg, VA. I would miss my songwriting partner. Working side by side while collaborating on a song can be stressful; working long distance as we had while I was overseas was even more difficult. Nevertheless, we vowed to give our new separation a try, at least to the extent time and obligations would allow.

In the meantime I needed a place in Manhattan to bed down and located a room in an upper West Side apartment off 145th Street. It was far from being fancy but the rent was good. There were three rooms for two boarders each on either side of a long hallway, one bath (no shower) and a kitchen. Each of six boarders was assigned a separate space in the cupboard for a fork, knife, spoon, two plates, a cup and saucer, and a plastic drinking glass. There were designated areas in the refrigerator and cupboard for food, to which identification tags were scotch-taped. Management provided pots, pans, and soap. Roaches were everywhere, compliments of the house.

Given this cozy atmosphere, a subway ride to just about anywhere in town was a welcome relief. In Times Square the sign on the Paramount Theater marquee read:

JONI JAMES WITH THE JOHNNY LONG ORCHESTRA

It wasn't often that I saw names of people I knew listed on marquees. On this one I was excited to notice two persons who were familiar to me: recording star and Paramount headliner Joni James was a classmate of my twin brothers in high school. She used to come to our house in Chicago and sing with us around the piano. Johnny Long was a fraternity brother from Duke University whose band played at DePauw University when I was there.

Joni had not arrived at the Paramount but I did have an opportunity to chat with Johnny. It was good to cross paths with him once again and to see how far he and his orchestra had come. They had three hit recordings to their credit, *Blue Skies, Sweet Sue,* and *Shanty Town.* At college I had spoken to Johnny of my desire to be a songwriter. Perhaps now, with at least one published song to my credit, he would be open to listening to some of my others.

Meanwhile I had an appointment to visit Eddie Fisher's manager Milt Blackstone. His office was just a few blocks from the Paramount.

"Yes," his secretary informed me, "Mr. Blackstone was expecting you, but he was called out of town. He's staying at the Grossinger Resort in the Catskills. You're invited to visit him there, if you happen to be up that way."

With nothing more than time on my hands I made it my business to just "happen to be up that way." My brother John went with me to keep me company. Grossinger was a popular spa and sports center that boasted its own airfield and post office. In its heyday it was home to a thousand guests a week. Supposedly Eddie Fisher made his singing debut there. We arrived late in the afternoon. Mr. Blackstone was at the rear of the facility watching Rocky Marciano train for a major boxing event. Seeing this great fighter mix it up with a sparring partner was an interesting experience for John and me.

We were prepared to spend the night at the resort but it didn't prove necessary as my meeting with Mr. Blackstone was short and sweet. He was well aware of my interest in obtaining a Fisher-Winterhalter recording of *Christmas Eve in My Home Town,* and asked if I would mind discussing the subject with him the following week in his Manhattan office. As we left the compound, John said he couldn't believe the meeting with Milt had been so brief, even a bit rude, having been invited there and then not talking business. It didn't bother me. I was satisfied the door to Eddie Fisher remained open.

From time to time I returned to my old haunts at NBC to make sure the company hadn't forgotten me and to ask my former colleagues to keep an eye out for any job possibilities. As slow as the process seemed, I never doubted the company's sincerity. I was confident that when the time came, someone would call. Until then I needed to stay focused on my songwriting and continue building relationships with publishers.

When Milt returned from Grossinger's I had my meeting. I wasn't in his office ten minutes when, to my surprise, we were joined by Colonel Johnson. I hadn't heard from my commanding officer since we were in Europe together. The colonel said he had just returned from a Public

Affairs meeting in Washington where a special *Army Hour* program was being prepared for our troops overseas. The program would include yuletide messages from our nation's top brass, including the Secretary of the Army Robert Stevens, Army Chief of Staff Matthew Ridgway, and a host of other dignitaries. I didn't know where all this was leading.

He then said the program would include a newly recorded performance of my song by Eddie Fisher with Hugo Winterhalter's Orchestra and Chorus! The news struck me like a bolt of lightning. The colonel had been the driving force in obtaining Eddie's recording for AFN in Europe, and now he was involved in this project. This was a major turn of events. It didn't take a crystal ball for me to realize that as Eddie Fisher's manager, Milt must have known about the recording when we were together at Grossinger's, but was cautioned not to say anything.

Colonel Johnson was now Commandant at First Army Headquarters on Governor's island in New York Harbor. Some days after our meeting in Milt's office he asked me to join him there. I arrived to find press photographers snapping pictures of Eddie presenting his new RCA recording to the colonel. I was then handed an Armed Forces press clipping dated November 19, 1953 which provided information on the projected *Army Hour* Christmas program. Next, I was shown a press kit prepared for editors of more than 1,300 Army, Navy, Air Force, Marine, and Coast Guard newspapers in the United States and worldwide. Essentially, I was told, this information would reach practically every person in the armed forces well before Christmas.

This was all well and good, but unfortunately it was already mid-November, too late in the season for RCA to release Eddie's recording here at home. And yet, as Mr. Blackstone had said the year before in Europe, "Well, it's a start anyway; maybe next year."

"Next year" seemed a long time away, but I was prepared to wait. Meanwhile, I needed to move on with my other music endeavors. In my pocket was an invitation from the American Society of Composers, Authors, and Publishers (ASCAP) to attend a formal membership dinner at the Waldorf Astoria Hotel. Vic Damone was the featured performer for the event. I was a huge fan. The story is told of how he began his career as an elevator operator at the Paramount Theater where singing star Perry Como was featured. He stopped the elevator mid-floor to sing to Como and to ask if he thought he had a good voice and if he should take singing lessons. Perry advised him to keep singing, which of course he did, and Damone went on to big things, even to seeing his own star on the Hollywood Walk of Fame.

I had not seen Vic since we were in Europe the year before. Believing it would be a good time to renew acquaintances I attended the ASCAP function. The evening almost slipped by, including an opportunity to chat with him. When he and his entourage headed for the elevator I made my way across the room to join them. I wish I had not done so.

The few moments in that confined space turned out to be very awkward, at least for me. Damone appeared to be deep in thought, his arms folded, his chin sunk into his chest. If he noticed me, he chose not to acknowledge it. Perhaps he was tired from the ASCAP event and the concentration his performance demanded. As the elevator reached the ground floor I reminded him of our get-togethers in Europe. Stepping into the hotel lobby his comment to me was, "Yeah, you shined my shoes."

Watching him and his group continue down the front steps, I wondered what could have sparked so snide a remark. I refused to believe it was because he chose not to record my Christmas song for AFN, while Eddie Fisher did. That seemed too petty. I was dumbfounded. This didn't make any sense. As I watched Damone's limo pull away from the Waldorf I felt betrayed and wondered what might be said of people who seek the approbation of others while habitually shooting themselves in the foot?

I was still without a job and living on meager army savings. Something had to give. I paid another visit to Joni James at the Paramount, showed her a couple of my songs, and we agreed to keep in touch. I then proceeded to Johnny Long's dressing room. His Paramount gig was coming to a close and the band would soon be doing one-night stands across the country. Johnny said he was going to lose his piano player, and asked if I would like the job. It was a very tempting offer. I felt I could handle Johnny's playbook of songs but felt I would be a weak accompanist for the male and female vocalists. Realizing the weight of such a responsibility, I thanked him for the offer and graciously declined.

A couple of days later Johnny's road manager contacted me to say they were losing their male vocalist and asked if I'd be interested in talking with them. As cautious as I had been about the pianist opportunity, for some reason I felt singing with the band was a better fit and so went back to the Paramount and auditioned. I sang three songs, finishing with one of Johnny's hit recordings, *Blue Skies*. Apparently that clinched the deal, as the road manager outlined the band's travel schedule:

> *We have dates up and down the coast and in between: Maine, New Hampshire, Vermont, practically all of the New England States. Gradually, we will work our way south to Memphis and a two-week stint at the Peabody Hotel. After that, we are looking at dates at Tinker Air Force Base in Oklahoma City, Fort Sill in Lawton, and then the US Naval Air Station in Corpus Christi. From there we cross Ole Miss and work our way through the Midwest. As you can see, the majority of our gigs are one-nighters.*

My head was reeling. I had never thought of myself as a band singer and now here I was being offered a chance to travel with one of the best in the land. The big question for me was whether I wanted to be living out of a trunk again, bedding down in different locales every night. I had not heard from NBC. Apparently there were still no job openings. When Johnny said he would pay me two hundred dollars a week, I took it. I actually looked forward to the new experience. When the manager handed me a copy of the band's itinerary, the deal was sealed.

Our big Carey bus was parked in front of the Paramount Theater in Times Square. On the side, in big, bold letters were the words, *THE*

JOHNNY LONG ORCHESTRA. To my utter surprise, the girl singer entering the bus was my friend, Barbara Hammond, a former member of the NBC Guide staff. I was aware that Barbara had a lovely voice, but never realized she harbored the remotest desire to sing with a band. Now, here we were, about to tour the country together.

I would soon learn that orchestra life was not for the faint at heart. In the weeks and months to follow I developed a great admiration for those who make their living on the road, separated from their friends and family for extended periods of time. The routine was this: finish an engagement, load gear and outfits into the bus, drive to the next town, check into a hotel, eat, and sleep, do the date. Next morning, re-board the bus, load up, drive to the next town, do the engagement, store the gear, drive to the next town, check into a hotel, eat, sleep, do the date.

In the 1950s and 60s there were no cell phones or Ipads or computers, but we did have jukeboxes. At every pit stop along our route the first order of business was to locate one and check out the current songs. It was as if the jukes were the relevant journals of the times, informing us as to who was recording what song. Sometimes we would hear a brand new recording and sometimes we would just enjoy listening to whatever had been on the charts for awhile.

There was one pit stop worth mentioning. It was located in the coal-mining district of Pennsylvania. We had finished a date and had traveled some distance when the band manager instructed our driver to pull into the first eating place he came to. We should have kept going. Instead, we stopped at a restaurant that would have made a hotdog stand seem like the Waldorf. It was a smoke-filled, dingy place where unshaven locals on bar stools looked like they had just escaped from prison.

As fifteen dressed-up dudes and a gal in a fancy evening gown entered the place, all eyes turned toward us. We did not survey the menu, such as it was. Instead, we all ordered the same thing, a hamburger, not rare or medium or well-done, thank you, just a hamburger and some fries and a cup of coffee. No thank you, no cream or sugar, just coffee. We asked no questions. As we sat there, we looked neither right nor left, nor did we speak in loud tones. No one looked around for a jukebox. Believing we were going to be eaten for dinner ourselves, we downed our food quickly, tipped extra heavy, and then left the place, happy to have escaped with our lives.

The Peabody Hotel in Memphis was a welcome respite from all the one-nighters. This engagement was for a full two weeks. Unfortunately for the boys in the band, they were required to do two sets a day, a tea dance in the afternoon and a dinner dance in the evening. Not so for Barbara and me. We lucked out, being required to do only the dinner dance. The Peabody had a radio station in the lobby and we did some interviews there, attended a couple of baseball games in town, and for two weeks generally enjoyed touring the historic city that gave birth to the blues.

After finishing the two-week gig at the Peabody we motored west in a heavy rain to catch a ferry boat across the Mississippi River. Next date: Arkansas. We had been on the road for quite a spell when our driver misread the map, left the main highway, and headed down a back road into farming country. We must have gone a couple of miles before he realized his mistake and decided to turn the bus around. In doing so he backed it into a ditch and there we were, stuck. Johnny and his wife Pat, following in their Cadillac convertible, instructed us to stay dry while they went looking for a tow truck or vehicle to pull us out.

Time passed ever so slowly. While the band kept warm on whatever they were drinking, I decided to go for help. Perhaps I might locate a farmer with a tractor. I took off on foot down a moonlit, muddy country road, finally coming to a farm house. Walking through the gate I was greeted by a not-too-friendly dog whose barking awakened the occupants. In another minute a porch light went on, and in the doorway stood a farmer with a double-barreled shotgun cradled on his arm, staring at a city dude all dressed up in a white dinner jacket and dripping like a sponge. Fortunately he was a kind old guy. After relating my story he agreed to see what our problem was and if he could be of any help.

With his shaggy dog barking behind us, I stood on the back of the huge tractor, arms around the farmer's waist, attempting to dodge the mud splattering into my face from the huge wheels. The band bus was about four blocks from his farm house. Forget my white jacket and new dress pants; by the time we arrived on the scene they were toast. The rain was still falling quite heavily and I was shivering uncontrollably when one of the band boys gave me a shot of brandy to warm my bones. The farmer chained his tractor to our bus and yanked it back onto the road as if it were a toy, accepting nothing as compensation for his help. He simply wished us good luck and, with his dog trailing behind, headed back to his farm, most likely pitying the lot of us. Our bus had just turned onto the highway leading to the Arkansas ferry boat when Johnny and Pat appeared with a tow truck.

A mid-June 1954 engagement at the Roseland Ballroom in New York City was the last time I would appear with the Johnny Long Orchestra. After three months on the road it felt strange to actually be back in New York singing in a Broadway nightclub. Johnny asked if there was any chance I would change my mind about leaving the band. I thanked him, but explained that I had to be where the action was, that every time our bus headed towards Manhattan I got goose bumps. Besides, I said, now he was free to find a vocalist who didn't sing off key.

AN EXCITING MOMENT

Eddie Fisher presenting his RCA recording of Christmas Eve in My Home Town *to AFN's Colonel Philip Johnson*

CHAPTER 12

The Eddie Fisher Saga

There are two types of people you meet along life's track, those who take all your strength from you, and those who put it all back.

—Anon

After leaving the Johnny Long Orchestra I accepted a job as a telephone sales agent with United Airlines in midtown Manhattan. Our government's *Army Hour* program to the troops the year before had been a huge success, and the Fisher-Winterhalter recording of *Christmas Eve in My Home Town* was received favorably as well. Now the question was, would RCA release the recording commercially to folks here at home?

I was working the phones at United when I received a call from an RCA Records marketing executive. He told me his sister had won an Arthur Godfrey talent contest the year before, and since I was able to book her on a flight home for Christmas he was returning the favor by phoning me. "I believe I am the bearer of good news," he said. "RCA has decided to release the Fisher-Winterhalter recording of your song. I have a copy of the official release sheet."

The news from RCA was almost too good to bear. Colonel Johnson had always believed that music had brought us together, and I had to share the news with him. After all, he was chiefly responsible for the recording. Sadly, my friend was quite ill and had been taken to the U.S Naval Hospital on Long Island. On the way to visit him I stopped off at the RCA Records building to pick up a copy of the RCA release sheet. In the hospital I found the colonel hooked up to a respirator and all sorts of tubes and IVs. An attending nurse said he wasn't capable of conversation and that Mrs. Johnson was on her way to the hospital.

I sat at the colonel's bedside for the longest time, finally removing the printed notice from my pocket. "Colonel," I whispered, "I have some good news. RCA is going to release our song on November fifth. I brought a copy of the RCA release sheet to show to you. We're record number fifty-five." I believe I detected something of a smile on the colonel's face. When Mrs. Johnson entered the room I bade goodbye to my friend, promised I would return, and left the hospital. I would never see him again. He passed away a short time later.

The following week I received a second phone call from the RCA executive. Something had gone wrong. The release had been cancelled, he said, and he didn't know the reason. He explained that he was present at the meeting when Christmas songs were being selected, and that the RCA brass liked the Fisher recording. Especially, he went on to say, they were impressed with the head start it had enjoyed over the previous two years. To launch the Fisher recording, RCA had mapped out an extensive nationwide promotional campaign. The question was, what happened?

Placing the RCA release sheet in my pocket, I left my United Airlines office and headed across town to the NBC Studios. Eddie was in his *Coke Time* dressing room when I greeted him with the surprising news that the Christmas release had been cancelled.

"I know," he said, "I stopped it. I'm tired of the song, Stan. Sometimes I get tired of a song right after recording it. This one has been around for awhile, and . . . "

I couldn't believe what I was hearing, and I held up my hands to stop him from saying more. Recollections of all the obstacles that had been overcome to bring the song this far simply got to me, and I lost it.

> *Do you have any idea how difficult it is to get a song off the ground, Eddie? How hard everyone worked on this one, broadcasting your name all over the world for the past two years? The massive press coverage you've received; the special Army Hour program in which you were featured? I am not saying that my song is another* White Christmas, *but it has been good to you. This release would have meant the kind of break a writer needs. And you sit there very casually and tell me you are tired of the song? Wonderful!*

Fisher responded by saying I was a good writer and that I knew where he stayed, at the Essex House off Central Park, and that I could always show him something else. This time, I asked:

> *What is it with you, Eddie? You have everything going for you, a great voice, amazing talent. I will say this much, if you want to sing any more of my stuff, you will need a heart. If you ever had one, pal, somewhere along the line you lost it.*

There was no response this time. My last words to Eddie Fisher were to congratulate him on his engagement to Debbie Reynolds and to wish him a successful marriage and a lot of kids. And then I was out of there, never to see him again. I left the RCA building and crossed Manhattan to 57th Street until I passed Sutton Place and reached the granny park and my favorite bench overlooking the East River. I needed to think. If this is what a songwriter's journey is all about, I was not sure I wanted to continue down that road.

Being a professional songwriter is probably the most exasperating part of show business because so many people are involved. Generally a song first goes to a publisher who may demand changes. Next it is reviewed by a recording artist's manager or producer. If it passes those tests it may reach the artist himself. This three-fold process can take a week, a month, or a year. If the song actually gets recorded, the writer must then sweat out a release date providing the song doesn't get bumped or put on the shelf for any reason, as mine did.

But let us suppose the song actually does get released. The writer is then at the mercy of the record company's marketing people, the nation's radio stations, the disc jockeys, and, of course, the buying public. It does not end there. In the final analysis it is up to the writer to ride herd on his song, to make sure it gets its chance, because no one is going to do it for him.

A publisher will rarely return a song to a writer once it has been published or recorded, because a published song adds monetary value to the publisher's catalog. I was able to have the publishing rights to my Christmas song returned because I had done a favor for the publisher at that time, Gower Music. Marvin Kane was Gower's general manager who was also personal manager to Adam Wade, a recording artist. I was instrumental in arranging for Adam to make a guest appearance on the Tonight Show, and Marvin remembered that favor. When I approached him to seek return of the publishing rights to *Christmas Eve in My Home Town* he asked if he could hold on to the song for one more year. If he was not able to obtain a new recording in that time, he said he would reassign the publishing rights to my company, Big Island Music, Inc. Marvin kept his word. From that time on I built the copyright myself, recording by recording, deal by deal, license by license, until it could stand on its own.

Basically, that is the writer-publishing cycle. It is my opinion that if a budding songwriter understands the odds for and against him, and accepts all these challenges going in, he or she will at least have a fighting chance for success. That is assuming, of course, that the writer has the absolute burn to succeed and the monetary resources to persevere.

As for Eddie Fisher's 1954 recording for RCA, it remained in the can for thirty-four years. It was finally made available to the American public in 1988 when *Readers Digest* included the recording in one of its

Christmas offerings. It's a shame, actually, because Fisher never had a Christmas song to identify with, as had Nat Cole and Bing Crosby and a few other major artists. When Eddie hit the high notes his voice rang like a bell, and Hugo Winterhalter's arrangement of *Christmas Eve in My Home Town* added a dimension few recordings have matched.

The upshot of it all is this: a record company plays a commanding role in which songs will or will not be released. Rarely, however, will it ignore the demands of one of its superstars. Why risk alienating one of its chief income-producing talents over the release of a Christmas song with so limited a selling season?

Although it may seem a bit harsh to say this, the reason RCA was able to release the Fisher-Winterhalter recording of *Christmas Eve in My Home Town* after so many years was because Eddie Fisher, no longer a force in the music business, had lost the power to stop it.

IF THERE'S A PIANO, STAN WILL FIND IT

Queen Mary songfest on the way to London to record music

Stan and record producer Jerry Plano

CHAPTER 13

Back to NBC and the Good Life

I do the very best I can, the very best I know how, and I mean to keep doing it until the end.

—A. Lincoln

Since I was earning a fair salary at United Airlines I began looking for a better place to live. A good friend, Eddie Layton, a talented organist who worked with me on some of my song demos, steered me to an upscale private apartment where I could get a room for eleven dollars a week. For an extra dollar a night I could join them for dinner, provided I notify the owners in advance. No overnight guests were allowed, and no visitors were permitted unless one of the owners was present. These factors taken into consideration, I considered myself fortunate and accepted the terms of occupancy.

The apartment was at 574 West End Avenue off 88th Street and belonged to show people Sidney Lee and Burt Milton. It was an attractive dwelling with a large foyer, a huge library, a reading room off the entranceway, and two living rooms, each with its own grand piano. Down the hallway past the kitchen was the *English Room,* which I shared with a fellow who worked on Wall Street. This twin bedroom had an adjoining bath connected to the *French Room* which was rented out to a Radio City Rockette. Sidney Lee and Burt's ornate bedroom was farther down the hall, the *Queen's Room,* which truly reflected the flamboyant nature of this colorful pair.

Show people were forever coming and going. During formal gatherings songwriters and entertainers would perform their specialties. Sometimes I was hired to serve cocktails at these functions. One evening noted composer and pianist Peter De Rose delighted guests by playing his well-known composition, *Deep Purple.* Peter was a gracious man who was known to give you the shirt off his back, which he did, actually. On one of his visits I admired a deep blue sport shirt he was wearing. The next day he had it wrapped and delivered to me by messenger.

Months later, on a busy day at United, I finally received the phone call I had been waiting for, one which would change the course of my professional career for the next twenty-two years. On the other end of the line was WNBC Station Manager Peter Affe, wanting to know if I would like to come back to work. There were two television job openings, he said, one as a Stage Manager and the other as an Associate Director.

"Which one pays more?" I asked.

The answer came back, "Associate Director."

"I'll take that one," I replied.

Thankfully, NBC was supportive of my music aspirations, especially as the company might be the beneficiary. In turn I maintained a proper balance between my music and my responsibilities to the network. When personal music projects presented themselves I pursued them on my own time, never infringing on official duties and not asking for special favors.

One of my overseas assignments for NBC was returning to Europe with news anchor Chet Huntley to cover the funeral services of Konrad Adenauer, the first chancellor of West Germany. It was a huge undertaking involving every major city in Germany. Boat flotillas and camera vessels participated along the Rhine River. Fifty-eight European countries were involved, with NBC serving as broadcast coordinator for the weeklong event. Later I covered space launches at Cape Canaveral and worked in talent pools with other outstanding reporters. One in particular was broadcast legend, Walter Cronkite. Still later, when NBC's President Pat Weaver launched the long-running *Today, Home, and Tonight* (*THT*) series of shows, I worked on them as well. I especially enjoyed assisting in the production of variety and dramatic specials.

My music projects were moving along nicely as well. Jerry Plano was Special Projects Director for RCA Records, and I was introduced to him. His RCA division compiled songs for albums. Jerry was an encyclopedia of musical knowledge. If a song was recorded Jerry knew its history, who published it, who wrote it, and the exact year of copyright. If a song entered public domain or was controlled by a writer's estate, he researched that information as well. Once selections were agreed upon he would acquire the necessary rights and permits and produce the album. Compilations continue to be a lucrative area for writers and publishers, and Jerry included *Christmas Eve in My Home Town* in many of his Yuletide albums throughout the years. He also arranged for two other of my songs, *Take Thou My Heart* and *Searching Wind,* to be recorded by Metropolitan tenor, Richard Tucker.

A very popular singing group was the four Paulette Sisters, Jane, Betty, Gloria and Barbara. Other singing groups of that era were the McGuire Sisters, The Andrew Sisters, and the Lennon Sisters, but my favorites were the Paulette Sisters. Their biggest hit for Columbia Records was *Glow Worm.* Another was *Never Smile at a Crocodile,* which was featured in the 1998 Meg Ryan–Tom Hanks movie, *You've Got Mail.* I had a crush on all four of the girls, especially Gloria ("Tootie," we called her) because she was so cute.

Whenever I was bored with the city, or hungry for a good home-cooked meal, or simply just wanted to hang out, I would take a subway train to their home in Forest Hills. Their mom was a kick, with a heartier laugh than the girls. Jane ("Doc," we called her) was the boss. She wrote *Eustace, The Useless Rabbit* with me, as well as her own Christmas perennial, *Santa Got Stuck in the Chimney*. To this day the Paulette Sisters remain some of my closest friends, real people, honest, fun, and loyal. I think of them often.

Music and work-wise and enjoying a well-paying job for the first time, everything was going well. I no longer felt compelled to rent a room in a boarding house and began searching for an apartment. My Wall Street roommate was anxious to make a move as well. Together we investigated an apartment on the corner of 84th and Riverside Drive, near the 79th Street Boat Basin on the Hudson River. There was a problem. The unit we were investigating was located at the rear of the apartment complex, with no view. "Little Joe" was the elevator operator of this eight-story, corner building and we asked him if he knew of an available unit overlooking the river. After eyeing us up and down to see if we would be good tenants, he took us up to the sixth floor. "The lady who lives in 6Y is going to move out," he said. "It's a corner apartment. Maybe she will show it to you."

It was winter and a heavy blanket of snow had fallen. When we entered the apartment the first thing we noticed was that every window in the circular living room faced the Hudson, with a view of New Jersey beyond. The Statue of Liberty was to the south; the George Washington Bridge was to the north. Although we technically could not see either of them, they made for good talking points. The rent for this apartment was three hundred thirty dollars a month unfurnished, a far cry from the meager rent we were paying on West End Avenue. I loved the place, especially the view, and so did my roommate. We said we'd take it. At least, that was the initial plan.

Sometime before the apartment was available my roommate backed out. He told me his mother didn't want him to live in the "wicked city" anymore, and that he was returning to Omaha. I was not too happy about that. Without his participation the rent would be a bit of a squeeze, but no matter. There was not an apartment like it anywhere in Manhattan, and I wanted it. A friend's uncle owned a furniture warehouse, and that's where I found everything I would need, including a small upright piano. When the apartment became available, I signed the lease and moved in.

There was always something interesting to see along Riverside Drive, no matter which window I looked out. In rough, sometimes hurricane force weather, I would witness expensive boats (even a classic Chinese junk) in jeopardy. On more than one occasion I would see beautiful yachts break their moorings and float, unmanned, down the river. In such cases I would phone NBC newscasters and suggest they instruct boat owners to come to the basin and attend their vessels. Had I been living in the apartment when Captain Sullenberger belly-landed his commercial airliner in the Hudson in 2010, I might have witnessed the amazing spectacle from my sixth-floor vantage point.

One evening an Army lieutenant in dress uniform appeared at my door. It was Brother Hap (Clifton) who had just been discharged from the service and came to visit me for the weekend. Eventually Hap took a job as account executive with United Airlines, attending to the travel needs of show business people and sports teams like the New York football Giants. When the team traveled, he attended to the needs of the executives' wives and their pets. Many wouldn't make a trip unless Hap was in charge of their itineraries. Everybody loved him. Known at United as "mister personality," Wellington Mara, owner of the Giants, presented him with a lifetime season pass to all its games.

Hap's weekend visit to my apartment lasted ten years! During that time we became what might be described as quintessential bachelors. Hap was popular with the stewardesses, always traveled first class, and took me with him. Hawaii was practically our second home. We bought land on the Big Island, flew to Tahiti, and visited exotic Bora Bora, the island paradise Michener wrote about in his book, *South Pacific.*

Between Hap's salary and mine we had enough cash to buy an eighteen-foot, mahogany, lap-strake boat, powered by a fifty-horsepower Johnson outboard. Compared to fancy yachts moored at the basin ours was a relatively small, albeit well-equipped, craft. When the weather was right, every weekend was party time on the boat. We played host to everyone - friends, family, and out-of-towners. Our Manhattan boat tours became legendary. Passengers on passing Circle Line boats eyed us with envy. While bathing beauties on luxurious yachts might be sipping cocktails, our ladies would be zigzagging on water skis behind our eighteen-foot runabout.

I was playing a sort of "girl-roulette" dating game, sometimes not all that successfully. On one occasion a Latin Quarter beauty brought her little son with her. On another occasion Hap and I invited half dozen Miss Latin America beauty contest winners to our place on Riverside Drive. That particular event didn't turn out very favorably either, as I ended up in the kitchen washing dishes with the chaperone.

After three years of running around I woke up to the fact that in chasing the fun I had lost the dream. I was totally unaware of what was happening in the world of music. "Rock and Roll" was here. *The Beatles* had invaded our shores, with waves of similar acts to follow. Most traditional songwriters were unfamiliar with the brand of music that had captured the imaginations of music lovers. Furthermore, they didn't know how to deal with it. In its wake, the "Big Band Era," as it had become known, slowly faded into the sunset. My own arranger, Jimmy Mundy, noted for his colorful arrangements for Tommy and Jimmy Dorsey, Count Basie and others, found it difficult to find work.

As the Rock and Roll invasion continued, a new breed of recording talent emerged that elected not to use their given family names. Instead, they called themselves "The Platters," "The Dominoes," "The Drifters." From my vantage point it appeared the music business, as I had come to know it, would never be the same.

If I didn't mind altering my writing style I might be able to stay in the game, but I did mind. My forte was being able to write strong melodies. People used to say that if you left a theater humming a tune it would be a hit because the melody would go to bed with you at night and wake up with you in the morning.

I was impressed with songs like *As Time Goes By,* the theme from the Bogart-Bacall movie, *Casablanca,* and *Lara's Theme* from the movie

Dr.Zhivago, and decided to concentrate my efforts in that direction. I came to learn that producers didn't really know what they wanted as far as theme music was concerned, or if they did they didn't know how to verbalize it. Once they were given the opportunity to listen to a finished product, however, that was a different story.

Borrowing the word "show" from show business, I decided to fund my own recording sessions and present my music to producers as a finished product. I was going to show them what I could do. I called it my "*Zabka do-it-yourself kit.*" Admittedly, I was acting on a hunch. Still, I felt there was a definite market for my music. Believing it was worth the investment, I took the plunge.

I went one step further. Johnny Mercer and a couple of other writers had been successful in forming their own company, Capitol Records, and I decided to do the same. While holding down my job at NBC, I launched Palladium Records in 1960. Brother Hap was still with United Airlines but joined me in selecting acts and producing records, as well as joining me on business trips. By acquiring master recordings from independent artists, plus signing and developing new ones, over a period of time we were considered respected, independent players in the record business. Our names appeared regularly in the music trade magazines *Cash Box* and *Billboard.* Within a two-year period Palladium Records had twenty-six record distributors in forty-eight states and Canada.

Meanwhile, I assembled twelve of what I considered my best songs and had them arranged for a large string orchestra. I felt that six of them might make good television themes. The remaining half dozen were big-band arrangements to be used as backing tracks for future Palladium vocalists. I gave all twelve songs to Jimmy Mundy to arrange, and then made plans to travel to England on the ocean liner, the *Queen Mary.* Recording costs were more reasonable in London, and a six-day ocean voyage would present ample time for me to check the music charts for possible errors or omissions.

Every day at a prearranged hour I went to work in one of the ship's passenger lounges. On the fifth day out, a pleasant Englishman introduced himself, saying he and his friends had observed me wading through this music every day. He went on to say that if I planned to record in London and needed some musicians, he and his boys were available. This distinguished gentleman was Johnny Dankworth, noted saxophonist for the great Ted Heath orchestra, Britain's most famous post-war big band. I was flabbergasted. Right then and there I hired the entire entourage.

We recorded at London's Phillips Studio. For the two-day session, I hired a conductor and thirty-seven musicians, which included the Heath band. Noted choral conductor Peter Knight led a vocal ensemble of ten singers. I worked the control room for both ten-hour recording sessions. When I returned home, four of my six instrumental themes were picked up by NBC, the first one being *Chimes,* the *Tonight Show* theme. A second version, *Chimes for Marching Band,* was later chosen as the official theme of *NBC Network Sports.* Although not a television theme as such, I wrote a third version, *Christmas Time Chimes,* with a sixteen-voice choir singing lines from traditional Christmas carols in counterpoint to the orchestra, similar to what was done by combining the two songs, *Moon Glow* and *Picnic.*

To sample *Chimes,* the *Tonight Show* Theme, the *NBC Sports* Theme, and *Christmas Time Chimes,* go to www.zabka.com

Palladium Records needed a success badly. Hap and I chose *Christmas Time Chimes* with the hope that Jack Paar would introduce the song on his *Tonight Show,* of which I was now an associate director. A network plug by this popular entertainer was vital to the success of the release. I didn't know Jack all that well personally, but his director, Kirk Alexander, was a good friend and presented the idea for me. Time passed slowly with no decision having been made. Still, Kirk assured me that Paar liked the recording but had not decided how to use it on the show. In the meantime, Christmas was just around the corner and time was of an essence. I had a plan, and ran it past another associate director, Hal Gurnee, who advised me to proceed with caution.

On a cold winter's night, a recording of the song in hand and restless for an answer, I bit the bullet and hopped a train from Manhattan to the Paar residence in Bronxville, New York. Snow was falling heavily, and the wayward wind was blowing the white stuff in wide, circular swaths against his front door. Jack answered the bell and said nothing; he simply stared at me. Besides being surprised, he was not happy that his home life had been interrupted. I thought I would at least be invited in from the cold, but obviously I had read him wrong; I had committed a major error in coming to his home uninvited.

As he often did when excited, Paar stuttered and asked, "Wha, wha, whatta ya doing here, pal?" Looking over his shoulder I could see his wife Miriam and daughter Randy warming themselves by the fireplace. Their furry dog cozy and snug at their feet, it was a scene right out of a Rockwell painting. Sensing Paar's restlessness, I explained my reason for the visit. "The Christmas recording, Jack. I was wondering if . . ."

Hastily interrupting me, he responded by saying he liked the song and was going to use it on his show. Then he asked how I was getting back to the city? I explained that a taxi was waiting. It was not. I had dismissed it. After Paar said goodbye and closed the front door I lingered on his porch wondering what television show I would be working on next. I shook my head, descended the winding steps, and then trudged through the wet snow to catch a train back to the city.

To my surprise, the very next night Jack introduced the song on his show by having the cameras pan the studio audience while the recording was being played over loud speakers. It was a huge success. Lights on the NBC switchboard lit up like a Christmas tree as callers wanted to know where they could buy the record. Kirk later told me the first thing Paar said to him when he came in that morning was, "Do you know what that S.O.B. did? He came to my house; scared the hell out of me. I thought he was bringing me my pink slip."

Jack Paar was a no-nonsense fellow, a quick-witted, clever, sensitive host, not given to idle banter. I gained added respect for him when I learned he had entertained my brother Al's First Marine Division on Guadalcanal during World War II. A few days after he premiered my song on his show he stopped me in a hallway to inquire how the record was doing sales-wise. "It's a good song," he said, "a nice recording, imaginative. Good luck with it." Actually, *Christmas Time Chimes* did very well until it was knocked off the charts by Harry Simeone's recording of *Little Drummer Boy.*

Sometime later, when Kirk Alexander left the *Paar Tonight Show* as Jack's director, my friend Hal Gurnee took his place. Airing a 105-minute show five times a week was a grind. After one particular disagreement over a "water closet" joke which NBC edited from a program, Paar walked off the show for three weeks. In March, 1962, "bone tired," as *TV Guide* described him, Paar left the show for the last time. In NBC's search for a replacement host the network was considering Jerry Lewis, Groucho Marks, Red Skelton, Joan Rivers, Joey Bishop, and a few more. Hal directed all these *Summer Specials* and I was his assistant. In the end, none of them were chosen to host the *Tonight Show.* Instead, NBC gave the job to Johnny Carson who was emceeing a television game show at ABC, *Who Do You Trust?* Johnny's brother Dick was directing the local *Soupy Sales Show* in Hollywood. When Johnny brought him to New York to direct his show, I stayed on as Dick's assistant.

Like Hal Gurnee before him, Dick was great to work with. From the very beginning I made it clear that I would assist him in any way I could. I explained that I had no desire to be a director, that I would introduce him to everyone he needed to know, and that I would endeavor to make his job as seamless and pleasant as possible. I believe our entire production and engineering staff felt that way; they were top drawer, fun people to be with. In the meantime, two more of my London instrumentals, *Searching Wind* and *Silhouette of a Dream,* were selected as themes for local NBC television shows.

Creatively and otherwise, I couldn't have been in a more desirable position, or so I thought.

It was that same year, 1962, that the government dropped a bombshell that profoundly affected the music industry. During an ongoing investigation the Attorney General's office cracked down on disc jockeys, especially the most popular ones, the so-called "Golden Gods" of the trade. Many were convicted of taking payola from promoters and record companies in exchange for airplay. Radio stations across the country were subject to a government consent decree. The result was that DJs no longer had a voice as to which records they could play. This function was now handled by either the station manager or a committee of radio station "decision makers."

That pretty much did it for Palladium Records. Under those conditions only giant companies like RCA, Columbia, and Capitol could survive. For small independents like ours that operated by releasing one record at a time and promoting it to the hilt by less aggressive tactics, the game was over, and Hap and I closed up shop. Our efforts produced at least three strong acts, *Lee Talboys, Barbara Lantz,* and a rock group from Denver, *The Astronauts,* the latter of which went over to RCA.

CHAPTER 14

Recording Sessions

The successful always have a number of projects planned, to which he looks forward. Any one of them could change the course of his life overnight.

—Mark Caine

We had just finished camera blocking in Studio 6B when I received an offer from Producer-Director George Schaefer, noted for his *Hallmark Hall of Fame* television series. George said he was developing a television special with a circus motif entitled *Turn the Key Deftly,* and wanted to know if I would consider writing the musical theme. His *Sunday Showcase Special* would star Julie Harris, Maximilian Schell, and Francis Lederer. George had a script sent to me with a note saying he was considering other composers, and once a decision was made he would be in touch regarding a shooting date. In the meantime, a friend suggested I write the theme while I was under no pressure. When completed, I played it for Mr. Schaefer and his associate producer, Bob Hartung, and demonstrated how variations on the theme could be used throughout the story. In the end I was offered the opportunity to write not only the theme but to score the entire production.

There were budget restraints. Only five thousand dollars had been set aside for writing, arranging, copying, and a small orchestra. Mr. Schaefer said I could use pre-existing music cues, but I was so pleased for the opportunity to work for him that I wrote every note myself and conducted the orchestra as well. There was no conflict with the *Tonight Show*. I was due for a vacation and used that time to work on Mr. Schaefer's *Turn the Key Deftly* production.

When Max Schell arrived from Switzerland to co-star in the show he came to my apartment a couple of times to relax and enjoy the river view. Over some freshly-made cheese fondue we talked at great length about his country, especially St. Moritz. He had skied there often, and was well acquainted with the resort. Max had a good singing voice and we spent some time around the piano. He liked the lyrics I had written to *The Key Theme* and asked for a copy of the words and music. I explained to him that the idea for using a waltz cadence for the theme came from listening to the song *Hi Lili, Hi Low*, from the movie *Lili*, starring his friend, Leslie Caron. Frank DeVol recorded a beautiful string rendition of *The Key Theme* for Columbia Records:

THE KEY THEME ©

Take me with you, wherever you go,
You hold the key to my heart.
Hold me near you, for I need you so.
Whisper that we'll never part.
You fill the empty,
You brighten my day,
You are the music where words want to play.
Take me with you, wherever you go,
You hold the key to my heart.

We taped *Turn The Key Deftly* live from NBC's Brooklyn studio, where an elaborate set had been built to house the large cast of principals and circus performers. The control room for Mr. Schaefer and his crew was in a studio adjacent to the sound stage. The announce booth was in another area. This was not an ordinary recording session in a controlled studio environment that I was used to. It was a Broadway-type theatrical production with live action taking place in a satellite studio while I conducted my orchestra over a television monitor.

I wasn't entirely happy with my performance. I don't believe Mr. Schaefer was either, although he never said as much. It seemed as though his associate director, Adrienne Luraschi, was constantly at my side with notes on music cues which I was already aware needed tightening. To fix trouble spots I paid the orchestra double time to continue rehearsing through lunch hour. There was no editing of the show. We did it live, in one take. What we laid down was what we got. Thankfully, all went well.

Recently I listened to my audio recording of the show and was pleased with what I heard. It was exciting to relive that moment in time and, over the opening theme to hear the voice of Mel Brandt announcing:

> *Now, from New York, the Breck Sunday Showcase presents,* Turn The Key Deftly, *starring Julie Harris, Maximilian Schell, and Francis Lederer, written by Alfred Bester, produced and directed by George Schaefer.*

With the critical success of *Turn the Key Deftly,* Mr.Schaefer added another Peabody Award to his string of credits, and the American Society of Composers, Authors and Publishers (ASCAP) presented me with my second of three Writer Awards.

These peer tributes did not go unnoticed by the *Tonight Show* Music Director, Skitch Henderson. I had been privileged to know and work with many talented people, but he was an exception. Privately I considered him someone who had reached the top with questionable ability and who exhibited an exalted presence that displayed his eminence. Increasingly resentful of my music exploits, it became clear that hostility was building over which I had no control. The stage was his, the control room was mine, and that's the way he wanted it to be. Under the circumstances, within the confines of my job I kept as low a music profile as possible when in his presence.

In truth, for some time I had been readying new songs to be recorded in Paris. Hap was always ready to travel, and when the time came, off we went. A dozen songs in hand, our destination was Eddie Barclay's Recording Studio in the Montmartre district. My plane fare was covered by NBC, as the *Tonight* producers wanted to tape some shows in Paris and asked if I would scout possible locations while I was there. Hap was the money manager. To cut expenses, I conducted the orchestra.

My arranger, Jimmy Mundy, was already in Paris recording an album with songwriter Bob Haymes. We used the same forty-three piece orchestra, booking the Barclay Studio for a full, twelve-hour day. That meant we would be recording at least one song an hour. Little did I realize the top condition a conductor must be in to support arms that are waving in every direction for so many hours.

Jimmy had completed all orchestral arrangements except one composition, *Take Thou My Heart*. Meanwhile, the recording date was quickly drawing near. Jimmy struggled for inspiration but just could not come up with a fresh idea. Three days before we were due into the studio he was propped up in his bed, music paper and pen at his side, sipping his favorite cognac, Reme' Martin. Not a note had been scribbled. Jimmy had earned a degree in electrical engineering, but instead chose music as a career. His knowledge of instruments, their range and physical capabilities, how each speaks and plays, with or against each other, could be learned. In Jimmy's case, this special gift came naturally.

He was a handsome guy. When he walked down the streets of Paris in his white, full-length leather coat, he was the spitting image of Duke Ellington. Jimmy's wife, Brucie, like Lena Horne, was strikingly beautiful. She and Jimmy were a close couple, and here in a Paris hotel suite Jimmy's mind was not in Paris. I asked him if he missed Brucie. "Why don't you phone her?" I asked. "I will leave the room and take a shower or something. Talk as long as you like. Put it on my bill."

I don't recall how long they talked, but Jimmy no sooner hung up the phone than he began writing. He simply needed to hear Brucie's voice and the inspiration came. The very next morning he handed me the arrangement. Whenever I listen to the Paris recording of *Take Thou My Heart*, recollections of that evening in Paris make me smile.

During the three-day lull before we started recording, Dick Carson and Bill Cosmos, *Tonight Show* production manager, arrived in Paris to check out the locations I had scouted. We toured the Latin Quarter, Le Lido, Montparnasse, and the Trocadero. Leaving the last for the best, we toured the Eiffel Tower off Avenue Champs Élysées. I had investigated it thoroughly and considered all pertinent logistics. Well known and easily accessible, taping the show from there was my favorite choice, and it was Dick's as well. In the end, the *Tonight* producers figured the time and expense in travelling the show wouldn't work, and so all plans were cancelled. Still, compliments of NBC, I got a free tour of Paris.

The recording date at the Eddie Barclay Studios arrived. I must tell you the story about one song, *Razz Ma Tazz*, which features the piano. Because it is such a crazy piece I felt it would be difficult to learn on the spot, and so I told Jacque, the piano player, not to be concerned, that I would play it myself. To keep my fingers limber I practiced *Razz Ma Tazz* every day before the recording session, not realizing how determined he would be to play the song. Every so often Jacque would pull out the arrangement of *Razz Ma Tazz*, prop it up on the piano, and run through it, seven or eight pages in all. He wasn't struggling so much with the notes as he was with the style and feeling of the song.

This was his solo! He was going to play this song, and that's all there was to it! I had to give him a chance. We laid down one take and then a second. Both renditions came off stiff, with no life. I didn't know how to handle the situation without hurting his feelings. Finally, my Paris music contractor, Eddie Adamis, took me aside. Sensing my frustration he said, "Stan, I know you can play your song, but you must understand, Jacque is the best jazz piano player in all of Paris. He wants to do this."

What to do? The clock on the wall indicated I was running out of recording time. It wasn't that *Razz Ma Tazz* was so difficult, only that it was written like a Czerny piano exercise with orchestral accompaniment, the notes covering the keyboard like a kitten on the keys. I was hoping for something swingy, something jazzy. Finally a thought came to me and I leaned down from the podium. "Jacque," I whispered, "Have you ever heard of an American piano player by the name of Fats Waller? You know, he wears this crazy hat and always has a cigarette in his mouth when he plays?"

His response was immediate, "Oh yes, Stan, Fats, sure. He's good. He swings." I glanced again at the time clock. My twelve-hour session was quickly winding down.

"Jacque," I said, "I'll tell you what I'm looking for. Fats throws a song away when he plays it, you know? He 'kicks it,' if you know what I mean."

He smiled. "Oh, yes Stan. 'Kick it.' I can do that!" And kick it he did. In one take! He did a masterful job, and the orchestra followed his lead with a jazzy, swinging accompaniment that ended our day's work in a gay, happy mood. Earlier, I had thumbtacks installed onto the hammers of a studio upright with the idea of recording a second, rinky-dink, piano roll version. But time had run out. Nevertheless, I was satisfied. Whenever I am at the piano today I play it as Jacque played it, although perhaps not as well.

The Paris recording session wouldn't be complete without relating how we recorded *Searching Wind*, technically my most challenging song and the one to which I had written both the words and music. It had been recorded twice before by string orchestras in New York and London, but I was never satisfied with either of the renditions and so asked Jimmy to do a third arrangement.

My First Violinist and Concert Master also played for the Paris Symphony. I didn't realize the respect an orchestra accorded a concert master. When he entered the studio forty-two musicians stood up to acknowledge his presence and members of the string section tapped their music stands in recognition. His Rolls Royce was parked outside. When the meter required dimes, one of the orchestra members did it for him. I believe the only task he undertook for himself was to pour his own wine and tear apart his own loaf of bread during recording breaks. Had I realized who I would be conducting, I am sure I would have felt intimidated. One thing I did know, I was fronting one big orchestra.

The music and lyric to *Searching Wind* are carefully wedded to each other. To understand why I wanted a good recording of the song is to know what the words say:

SEARCHING WIND ©

Searching Wind,
In your journey to all places
Will you linger with my love
If you see her 'long the way?

Searching Wind,
Will you whisper where she's waiting
Of the yearning in my heart
To be by her side one day?

Long, in the twilight hours I wander,
Cov'ring the sands and dark'ning shore.
Tell her a sad and lonely lover
Dreams of returning to wander no more.

Searching Wind,
All my life and all my soul are in her keeping.
Even now, as the stars leave the sky,
Speak of my love,
Searching Wind.

The last eight measures (above) are a violin solo that speak the closing words of the song. We did three takes of *Searching Wind.* Feeling the last performance was the best, I left the studio to join Hap,

Jimmy, and Eddie in the control room to listen to the playback. Surprisingly, the Concert Master followed us, his violin tucked securely under his left arm, his bow in his right hand, pressed firmly to his chest. A distinguished gentleman with a strong face and ready smile he carried himself with great assurance, yet addressed no one. His head tilted slightly upward, his eyes partially closed, he simply stared straight ahead and waited patiently for the playback. Tapping my shoulder to get my attention, Eddie whispered, "Stan, this man never comes into a control room. He doesn't care what he records. He must be quite interested in this piece."

When the playback was over, I glanced in the master's direction. *What did he think? Was he satisfied?* The last eight measures of *Searching Wind* were his solo, the part he came into the control room to listen to. Before reentering the studio he paused at the door. Turning to us, he said in French: "Pas rien. That is nothing. I can do better!"

We recorded the song one more time, the maestro playing the notes as if he had written the words himself. I glanced in his direction to determine his response. A positive nod of his head and a contented smile convinced me he was satisfied. This master violinist made the selection. If he was happy, I was happy. One thing I came away with was a broader and more intimate knowledge of the music business, especially the dedication of musicians to their craft. Whether I would have an opportunity to conduct so large an orchestra in the future was not clear. But of one thing I was certain, directing an orchestra is a demanding job, not cut out for amateurs, and the man waving the baton had better be in good condition to conduct over a twelve-hour stretch.

Back on the *Tonight Show* it became immediately clear that my French experience did not set well with Skitch Henderson. In taping a show, communication between the associate director in the control room and the music director on the set is vital. When I returned from Paris this important link became almost nonexistent. It was a struggle to get Skitch to accept my music cues except as relayed through the stage manager. When I needed to speak with him during the show he often would not pick up his head set. I wondered where this attitude was leading. Call it jealousy, envy, indifference, or what you will, this was not a healthy atmosphere.

Over a period of time, *The Tonight Show* became known as *"The Johnny Carson Tonight Show."* Soon thereafter NBC transferred Nancy Heimert from her job as commercial coordinator on *The Merv Griffin Show* to be our production assistant. Her assignment was to work closely with Dick, our two producers, four talent coordinators, and the music department in prepping shows for rehearsal and broadcast.

NBC's Standards and Practices Division monitored shows closely in those days. A big part of Nancy's responsibility was to take shorthand notes of everything that was said on the set during taping. In the event of controversy or a complaint, the producers would then refer to her notes and, if necessary, we'd find ourselves in the videotape room erasing any contested areas.

Besides being totally dedicated to her job, Nancy's outgoing personality made her very popular around the office and, as someone was quick to point out, she was "easy on the eyes." I had a standing rule never to date anyone from the company, but eventually chucked that idea by inviting her to dinner. Once in awhile after a show we would meet for a cocktail at Hurley's, a favorite gathering spot for NBC personnel. Occasionally, we would double date with Hap. I played all twelve string arrangements of my Paris recordings for her and she loved them, especially *Searching Wind* and *Razz Ma Tazz*.

One evening our *Tonight* trumpeter and flugelhorn player, Clark Terry, was performing at O'Henry's Steakhouse in Greenwich Village and I asked Nancy if she would like to join me and catch his show. That is when I learned we had more than music in common. Besides having majored in radio and television, I discovered she had studied dancing, performed in community players shows, and had sung in many high school and college choruses. More especially, she was a wonderful listener, an "encourager" with whom I felt comfortable in sharing my innermost thoughts and plans. We talked until wee hours of the morning. Eventually, we closed the place.

From that night on there was no looking back. Actually, I believe it was my boat that won her over. We especially enjoyed weekends circling Manhattan or challenging *Hell Gate*, the turbulent waterway connecting the East River with Long Island Sound. Storms didn't seem to bother Nancy. She preferred the rough over calmer waters. When taking the wheel she headed into the highest waves, her big smile beaming and blonde hair blowing in the wind as she hit them straight on. Our favorite destination was Huntington Harbor on Long Island's North Shore where my sister Georgia would meet us and drive us to her house for a barbeque and a swim. It always added to the fun when brother Hap and his date-of-the-month would join us for the weekend. On our return to Manhattan we would dock the boat, wash it down, and close her up. That finished, the four of us would head to the apartment and our favorite dinner of fried chicken and barley from a nearby Broadway deli. We savored the smell of that tasty morsel all the way home where a fresh shower, followed by a cocktail and some relaxing music had become an after-boating ritual.

One afternoon as Nancy and I were finishing lunch at a Broadway cafe, Hap stopped by to join us. Nancy could not stay, as she needed to return to the studio. Watching her disappear into the crowd Hap said, "Hoagy, when are you going to marry that girl?" I told him I had promised Mom I would watch out after him, and that it turned out to be a full-time job.

The joy in our relationship was clouded with sad news on Friday, November 22, 1963. We were in camera rehearsal when Nancy, visibly upset, entered the studio uttering the words "Dallas" and "the President." Soon we learned that John F. Kennedy had been assassinated. All activity in Studio 6B came to a halt. On a television monitor overhead someone had piped in a CBS television feed of Walter Cronkite detailing a running account of the event.

No one knew what to say, or if they could believe what they were seeing on the screen. Johnny entered the studio with his brother and our producer and told everyone to go home. The show was cancelled for the day.

I escorted Nancy back to the office where we found our associate producer John Carsey shaking, as if he were cold. We felt he shouldn't be alone and so we hailed a taxi and accompanied him to his Greenwich Village apartment. Neither Nancy nor I cared to be alone either, and so we went to my place on Riverside Drive. Throughout the night and weekend we followed television accounts of the tragic events unfolding in Dallas.

I had met John Kennedy in person when he was running for president. The occasion was a fundraiser at the Roosevelt Hotel in New York that NBC News assigned me to cover. I remember Jackie, the candidate's wife, offering him a glass of water and wishing him well before he was to deliver his speech. Watching him pace the floor backstage, I recalled his heroic exploits in the Pacific as commander of a patrol boat. He seemed like one of my brothers, a regular fellow, young and energetic. Along with these obvious attributes, there was something special about John Kennedy's persona, something about his eyes that was captivating, something in his demeanor that made me feel he just might be elected and go on to become a good president.

Unfortunately, he was not allowed a decent opportunity to prove himself. After only a thousand days in office, at age forty-three, John F. Kennedy was gunned down by an assassin's bullet, the youngest president to serve our country and the youngest to die. Our country had lost one of its most beloved presidents in a manner that defied all logic.

In the meantime, as Skitch Henderson's true colors became transparent, all was not well on the Tonight Show stage. Because of my musical background I was perhaps more sensitive than others on the staff with regards to his haughty attitude toward guests of less-than-star status, and it irked me. I had always made it a practice never to judge or speak harshly about anyone. Inwardly, however, I considered Henderson a transparent foil for Johnny, someone who sought the acceptance and approbation of famous and talented performers like Count Basie, Bette Midler, or Joe Williams. With rare exception, Skitch appeared almost aloof to newcomers who sought the encouragement someone in his position might have offered.

Although her account may differ, I remember when newcomer Barbra Streisand made her first guest appearance on the show. Riding the crest of a hit recording, waiting patiently for the rehearsal to begin, she seemed restless, almost uncomfortable. In an attempt to be friendly, and to make her feel at least welcomed, I asked Barbra if I could offer her a glass of water or a cup of tea. She politely declined. Skitch eventually made his entrance down the studio steps, greeted the orchestra, shuffled through some music on the piano, finally acknowledging her presence. He rehearsed Miss Streisand only once before camera blocking, never asking if the tempo was right, if she was comfortable, or if she had any questions. Had she been the big star of later years, his attitude would have been entirely different.

In previous years a sparkling array of talent had emerged from the NBC Guest Relations ranks: Steve Allen, Dave Garroway, Regis Philbin, Disney CEO Michael Eisner, Gordon MacRae, Kate Jackson, Bill Dana, Eva Marie Saint. I was successful in arranging an audition for Barbara Hammond, a former NBC Guidette and vocalist with the Johnny Long Orchestra when I sang with the band. Barbara was now angling for a recording contract and needed a boost in her career. A guest appearance on *The Johnny Carson Tonight Show* might well have been the break Barbara needed.

When her audition day arrived, our show's exalted music director examined her wardrobe and greeted her with the back-handed comment, "Who designed your outfit, a bag lady?" With that, not having sung a note, embarrassed and holding back tears, Barbara walked off the set. Sadly, she passed away sometime thereafter, the victim of a serious illness.

I had worked on the *Tonight Show* beginning with the first host, Steve Allen, and then Jack Paar. As much as I appreciated the creative freedoms I enjoyed, the fine associations with outstanding crews, I found the atmosphere on the *Carson Tonight* set and around the office becoming more untenable than I could bear. From time to time our producer, Art Stark, cautioned me that he had not hired Henderson and that he could not fire him. Somehow, he said, I needed to arrive at some accommodation with him.

While I felt I had made that effort on more than one occasion, the insult to my friend Barbara Hammond was impossible for me to accept. The *Carson* crew was a talented and energetic team of high achievers, and I felt the tension between Skitch and me was muddying the waters. Visiting Johnny in his office, I suggested it might be better all around if I left his show.

Mr. and Mrs. Stan Zabka

CHAPTER 15

Mixing Marriage and Music

Strange, my desire for certain pleasures is part of my pain.

— Kahlil Gibran

On the romantic side things weren't looking much better. Not only had my long association with the *Tonight Show* come to an end, but the relationship between Nancy and me had become somewhat blurred. If I had managed to skirt the long-term implications of our steady dating, she had not. Whether by design or experiment, there was no confusion on her part. She simply made herself unavailable.

When even my phone calls went unanswered, I took the elevator to the seventh floor of NBC where the *Tonight Show* control room was located. The show was on a commercial break when Nancy looked up from her work to see me staring at her through the double-glass windows, "like a lost puppy," as she later described it. I needed to see her.

After the show we went to O'Henry's Steakhouse, the familiar spot in Greenwich Village where we first dated. Conversation was a bit strained at first. Words didn't come in an easy way. Both of us knew why we were there.

Nancy's birthday was nearing, and I had written a song for her that expressed my feelings. I watched her reaction as she read the words:

WHAT'S HAPPENED TO ME? ©

Don't know What's Happened To Me,
What makes me feel like I do,
Can I be falling in love?
I wish I knew.

Don't know What's Happened To Me,
This mood is so hard to hide,
I'm even blushing inside,
Don't laugh, it's true.

If it's not love, then why should I care
If there's someone else sharing the wine?
If it's not love, tell me why should I want you
for mine, all mine?

I just need to know
What sort of chance there might be,
That this is happening to you,
What's Happened to Me?

A period of silence followed. Nancy just looked at me as if wondering what was to follow. More silence. The moment of truth had arrived. It was not the most romantic means of proposing, I suppose, and it might have been presumptuous on my part, but placing a diamond ring on her finger, I asked what she would like for her birthday. What she wanted, she said, was me, and my baby.

"Tonight?" I asked.

"No, silly," she replied, "After we are married."

The die had been cast, and I asked Nancy to set the date. One important element remained, however. Although she knew my brothers Hap and John, and my sister Georgia, she had never met my mother or other members of my family. And so, during a hiatus from our jobs, we flew to Chicago.

We arrived at brother Frank's and his wife Gerry's house on the South Side. Brother Lucky (Clifford) and his wife Joyce were there as well. Knowing Lucky was a dentist, Nancy played a joke on him by blackening one of her front teeth with mascara and greeting him with a clown-like grin. Hearing the laughter, Mom beckoned us to join her in the living room. Because of her diabetes and resultant glaucoma, Mom had lost her sight. Even so, she had not lost her sense of humor. As Nancy sat down beside her, Mom placed a hand on Nancy's thigh and, nodding her head in approval, smiled and said, "Well, she is a healthy one anyway."

After receiving Mom's blessing we flew back to New York to scout around for a place to be married. We attended church at Fifth Avenue Presbyterian, but it was too big. We wanted something less pretentious. Midtown on Park Avenue was a lovely Byzantine-style church, just what we were looking for. In the lobby was a bronze sculpture of Ralph W. Sockman, Minister Emeritus and number one Protestant radio pastor in the U.S. I attended a Methodist college and knew of this distinguished pastor. When he was still active in the ministry so many people attended his morning sermons that he repeated them in the afternoon. People called them *Sockman Sundays.*

While discussing our wedding plans with a junior minister he asked the name of the pastor who would be conducting the service. Hesitantly I offered the casual remark that we had not chosen one, but that it would be great if Dr. Sockman would consider performing the ceremony. Needless to say, we were totally shocked by the young minister's response: "You know," he said, "the doctor claims that since he retired no one asks him to perform marriages anymore. I think he would be delighted to do it."

We were married August 2, 1964. The sanctuary was scented with decorative flowers, the wedding party looked especially handsome, and the bride was never more beautiful. Hap, my best man, was in great voice as he sang my wedding song, *Take Thou My Heart.* Waiting for Nancy and me at the altar, white-haired Dr. Sockman was an imposing figure in his colorful, ornate robe. After a few opening words, the Bible clutched firmly in weathered hands, he read a few lines from scripture. When it came time to exchange vows, and his eyes searched mine, I felt as if I were appearing before Moses incarnate. Then came the words, "Repeat after me." I could not. I simply stood there as if in a state of shock. Nancy later claimed the silence lasted long enough for her to consider how she would leave the church gracefully. She recalls squeezing my hand for encouragement and how Hap moved in behind me, believing I was going to faint. The words "I now pronounce you" still resound loud and clear in my ears.

Following the wedding ceremony we had a reception at the *Tavern on the Green* in Central Park. It was a gala affair which Nancy personally arranged. Before leaving the church, Hap placed some champagne in our limo, and Nancy and I toasted the universe as we took two or three spins around the park, savoring the moment by ourselves. Little did we realize that trailing us was a parade of cars with out-of-town guests who thought we were heading to the reception.

Hap kept the Riverside Drive apartment (and the boat) and Nancy and I moved into a twenty-fifth floor apartment in the *Pavilion,* a new midtown complex overlooking the East River. As one of the first tenants in the building we were fortunate, as our rent remained about the same as on Riverside Drive, an unbelievable $330 a month. Our living room was large enough to hold a piano, and I purchased an African mahogany, Steinway-A Grand which we later sold when we moved to Los Angeles. I wish we had not. It was a beauty, with great tone. Besides, they don't make them anymore, and a used Steinway-A is hard to find.

Among the array of wedding gifts the most generous (and certainly the most unexpected), was from my former boss Johnny Carson who asked if I would like to premier my theme album on his show. Because of the long-standing animosity that existed between the music director and me, the *Tonight* producer had to do some maneuvering and book me on the show when Skitch Henderson was out of town. The date that was set was September 1, 1964.

While I was no longer Johnny's associate director, Nancy stayed on as production assistant. As I was introduced, a recording of my *Tonight Show* theme, *Chimes,* was aired. It felt strange making my entrance onto the stage through the big red curtain. How many times had I witnessed other acts doing the same? At the piano I sang and played *Noreen,* led the orchestra in *The Key Theme,* and concluded with my keyboard rendition of *Razz Ma Tazz.*

I was about to leave the stage when Johnny joined me at the piano. I had a feeling he was up to something, as he had a big smile on his face. Shading his eyes with my record album he looked past the audience and asked if Nancy was upstairs in the control booth. Then he jokingly said: "Stan left the show to marry my brother's secretary. I guess that makes my brother, my aunt."

When Ed McMahon asked Johnny if a person had to leave the show to get married, Johnny's reply was, "Yes. We don't want any happy people around here."

Johnny Carson and me on the Tonight Show

The title of my album is, *The Paris Strings Play Zabka's Themes From Television.* I still have Johnny's original, coffee-stained liner notes and believe he was more than generous with his comments:

> *It is always somewhat risky writing a few notes about one of your friend's accomplishments; some are bound to feel you are overstating the case. Not so with Stan Zabka. Stan, the former Associate Director of the* Tonight Show, *is a talented man. And that's rarer than you might think in this era of the "overnight star" with his hit record. Stan has set down some music to listen to, not be assaulted by. In little less than eight weeks the current 'top ten,' or whatever they call them now, will be forgotten, noisy interruptions. But a good musical composition, like a good wine, is not an ephemeral thing. So, as you would enjoy a good wine, become acquainted with these original compositions by Stan. You'll find them a welcome change, and who knows, along with discovering a new talent, you might discover a good new wine.*

Johnny's good nature and encouragement to his guests, no matter their station, are legendary. One of the songs in my album was *Take Thou My Heart* which my brother Hap sang so beautifully at our wedding. I originally wrote it for a former Page Boy roommate Perry Massey when he got married. Aware that Nancy was watching us in the control room on the floor above, I asked Johnny if it would be okay if I recited the words to her. He said, "Sure."

TAKE THOU MY HEART ©

Take, Thou, My Heart for thine.
Take every dream fashioned there.
Take every hope, every thought divine,
The deep, tender love it would share.
Humble, unworthy, to stand at thy side,
No secret I hide, unbeknown.

Take, Thou, My Heart for thine,
For thine, now, is mine alone.

"You must be in love with your wife," Johnny said.

"I am," I replied.

I exited the stage the way I came in, through the big red curtain. Thoughtfully, Dick Carson had arranged for my performance to be taped, and presented me with a copy. I'm fortunate to own it, as NBC destroyed all the tapes of Johnny's early years. My performance may be the oldest surviving recording of *The Tonight Show Starring Johnny Carson*. From this 1964, two-inch quad tape, David Crosthwait of DC Video in Burbank was able to strike digital copies. According to David, the color, and sound quality in particular, were excellent, enabling him to digitize and preserve this performance as if it were a new show. That is pretty amazing after all these years. Among the treasures of my early days, this video is unquestionably my favorite.

To view the Carson video go to www.zabka.com

The years I was privileged to work with the Carson brothers are some of the most memorable and enjoyable that I can recall, both personally and professionally. As his associate director and sometimes foil I was a guest on Johnny's show on three different occasions, once being called from the control room to join him at his desk to assist in a gag. While I have a photograph of that moment, the exact nature of the gag escapes me. I believe it had to do with a carton of cigarettes. At least, that's what the photo shows.

A month or so after I had left the *Tonight Show* I received a phone call from Skitch Henderson's talent agent, Gary Nordino, at the William Morris Agency. Apparently Skitch felt he no longer needed an agent, or did not care to pay one, and so broke off the relationship. Gary offered to represent me as musical talent in his place, but I respectfully declined his offer since I would have had to leave NBC and enter a freelance world of which I was unaccustomed. The plain truth is I didn't see myself as a music director. I simply wanted to be a songwriter. My job with NBC had allowed me to pursue that goal, besides which I was reluctant to relinquish the monetary security my associate director job represented.

As for Henderson, it is my understanding that he eventually stepped on his own foot and was dismissed by the network under less than honorable circumstances. When he left *The Carson Tonight Show,* Doc Severinsen took his place as music director and stayed on until Johnny retired.

With no particular show assignment I was now relegated to working rotating schedules between NBC's news, sports, and special events divisions. Occasionally I would be assigned to Broadcast Operations Control (BOC), a television switching central. In an even less creative vein, oftentimes I would find myself with a stop watch laboriously timing commercials or programs in an isolated viewing booth.

Sometime during 1966 I learned that my friend Scotty Connal was creating an opening film for NBC Sports and liked my recording of *Chimes for Marching Band.* Sports Vice President Chet Simmons liked it as well, and before I knew it I had another music theme to my credit. Unfortunately the project became sidetracked while creating animation for the film. Week upon week seemed to drag by with no word from Scotty as to the film's status.

In the meantime Nancy was pregnant, had left *The Carson* Tonight Show, and was now working for Scotty and Chet. Even she could not determine what was causing the bottleneck. With the theme possibility foremost in mind I was not comfortable sitting back idly, waiting for something to happen. Restless for an answer, I would slip into Scotty's office while on night duty to see if an encouraging memo might be lying on his desk, something he hadn't shared with me.

Finally, magically, all the pieces came together and the film animation design was approved by the bosses. Once completed, my recording was dubbed in and the film was mailed to all NBC affiliated stations around the country. I was now co-composer of *Chimes,* the *NBC Net-*

work Sports Theme. When all was said and done I had to confess to Scotty that I had taken the liberty of entering his office at night and nosing around for information. I apologized for doing so, but he said it was okay, that it didn't surprise him. I'm not entirely sure what he meant by that, but I do know I was fortunate to work with a host of creative and talented people, and Scotty Connal was among them.

My friend fell ill during the 1996 Atlanta Olympics and passed away soon thereafter. I am positive I would have no detractors in declaring that sports programming was not quite the same without that talented, loveable man. When he and Chet Simmons left NBC they ran ESPN, the sports network that is alive and growing to this day. Scotty's children continued in the business, a talented sports family. I wonder if any of them learned to play hockey as well as their dad.

An interesting aside to the sports theme story concerns Tom Foty, a well-known network reporter and commentator in Washington, DC. Tom presented me with his off-the-air recording of an *NBC Special,* the 1967 broadcast of *Super Bowl I* (not called that in those days), between the Kansas City Chiefs and the Green Bay Packers. Famed sportscaster Curt Gowdy was the game announcer. The music behind his unique voice was my theme, *Chimes.*

Audio recording techniques were not all that sophisticated in the early days and I asked Tom how he was able to record the program off the air. He said he simply attached two audio clips to terminals in the back of his radio and connected them to a small wire recorder he used for tracking news events.

Along with the *Carson Tonight Show* tapes that were destroyed, the *New York Times* listed Foty's recording of the *NBC Special (*Super Bowl I*)* as one of television's "lost treasures." Tom said his recording is now safely ensconced in the *New York Museum of Radio and Television.*

BILLY ZABKA'S FIRST FILM ROLE, AGE FIVE

War Games, Vietnam Era, Port Washington, NY

CHAPTER 16

The Kate Smith/ Vietnam Connection

Of course it was a righteous war. My son fell in it.

—Anon

In November of 1955, US combat forces in Vietnam were committed to a war that would end twenty years later with the fall of Saigon. Five members of Nancy's and my extended families were serving in Vietnam and naturally we were concerned for their safety. Her brother-in-law was a pilot. One of my sister Sylvia's boys was in the Navy and another was in the Marines. Brother Bob's eldest boy was patrolling the Mekong Delta in a Navy gunboat, and his daughter's husband was a pilot.

During the 1960s the Viet Cong had built underground tunnels in Vietnam from which to wage war. When I moved to Los Angeles a writer named Buddy Reyes came to me with his screenplay, *Tunnel Rats,* the story of how volunteer Infantrymen performed search and destroy missions to clean out these tunnels. It was a dangerous mission, as the tunnels were booby-trapped, with the enemy hiding in dark places. In his studio were table models of the Viet Cong's elaborate below-the-surface training grounds, living and eating quarters, hospitals, and ammo storage areas. On Buddy's wall were pencil-sketches of narrow gauge railroads and switching centers for moving men and equipment through a virtual underground city from which the enemy could emerge at will, strike, and disappear.

Buddy's screenplay interested me and I signed on as a partner to help him mount the project and seek development funds. I soon learned that securing finances for a movie demanded more time and effort than I had envisioned, and expertise of which I had little knowledge. For prospective investors to routinely become excited in the film and then suddenly disappear was exasperating, and efforts exhausting. I found no way to continue my involvement and eventually had to exit the project. Buddy continued on his own until he himself had to let it go. A *Tunnel Rats* film eventually was made in Europe, but it didn't measure up to our concept in any way, shape or form.

In 1966, Kate Smith recorded *Christmas Eve in My Home Town* and made it the lead single of her RCA Christmas album. Explaining that she also wanted to do "something special" for our troops in Vietnam, Kate asked me to join her at her apartment and to bring a tape recorder and some blank tapes. In two hours she recorded thirty-six individual Christmas messages to our fighting men and women, wherever they were stationed around the world. I have never heard a warmer greeting to our troops, either before or since:

> *Hello, boys and girls, this is Kate Smith coming to you via Armed Forces Radio with a greeting to let you know that we are all thinking of you. I have recorded a song especially for you that was written by a couple of ex-GIs, Stan Zabka and Don Upton, and you will be hearing it soon. Its title is* Christmas Eve in My Home Town. *And boys and girls, Christmas won't be the same in your home town without you, but you can bet that you will be thought of and prayed for and loved just as much as if you were all here. I would like to say Merry Christmas to you, and may God bless you all.*

After recording these messages Kate phoned RCA with instructions to book her on both the *Johnny Carson Tonight Show* and Bing Crosby's *Hollywood Palace.* I have audio and video copies of her appearance with Bing Crosby. Regretfully, I have only an audio recording of her visit with Johnny Carson. Neglecting to have ordered a video copy was a huge oversight on my part. Kate explained to Johnny how she had been searching for songs for her new Christmas album when she found PFC Eddie Fisher's rendition on the desk of her record producer. Kate then told of how she took the recording to her home in Lake Placid, listened to it, and then told her producer it was a lovely song and to please include it in her RCA Christmas album. Johnny's reply was, "We could never find Stan. He was always running around the building somewhere, putting records on peoples' desks."

I have vivid recollections of those times, waiting for songs to be recorded, then released, only to see entire projects put on hold or fall through the cracks. The Eddie Fisher saga is still indelibly etched in my brain. Until Kate actually recorded my song I was fearful *Christmas Eve in My Home Town* would suffer the same fate. Days and weeks passed with no word as to whether a recording session had been scheduled or even if an orchestral arrangement had been commissioned. Sal Gelosi was Kate's confidant and chauffer who often came to me to obtain guest passes to the *Tonight* show. Sal kept me up to date as to what was happening. "Not to worry," he would assure me, "she likes the song. It's going to happen. Relax."

When I saw *The Kate Smith Christmas Album* actually displayed in a Broadway record store I was unable to contain my enthusiasm. To realize my song had been recorded by our country's greatest lady of song, the lady who introduced our greatest anthem, *God Bless America,* written by possibly our country's greatest songwriter, Irving Berlin, the moment was overwhelming! In a spurt of total exhilaration I walked out onto Broadway, raised my arms in the air, and in a loud voice shouted "I did it! I did it!" Not a single head turned. If passersby noticed or heard me, or even cared, they paid no attention. That's New York for you. One person, a drifter, did respond. He approached me from the shadows of a subway station and asked if I wanted to buy a watch.

Kate and I maintained a cordial relationship until she passed away in 1986. A devout Catholic, she and two Sisters from her parish were close friends. When Kate wanted to chat with me, but was ill or otherwise indisposed, she would ask one of them to place the call. Fond recollections of Kate were rekindled in 2001, the fiftieth anniversary of the publication of *Christmas Eve in My Home Town,* when Richard K. Hayes of the Kate Smith Commemorative Society invited me to Lake Placid to be guest at a festival being held in her honor. To be numbered among those Kate Smith called her friends is special.

Professionally, when someone of her stature records a work other artists or their managers check it out. That is how Nashville record producer Billy Sherrill found my Christmas song for Bobby Vinton, and how Jim Nabor's producer and others learned of it. In Kate Smith's case, it all started with her having discovered the Eddie Fisher recording on her producer's desk.

In the meantime, Nancy's and my family was growing. Our second child, Judith Marie, was just six weeks old and Billy was almost twenty months old when we moved from our Manhattan apartment to a home on Long Island. It took a year and a half to find a town where we wanted to raise our kids. I even went so far as to investigate areas in a helicopter, up and down the Jersey shore, the Hudson River, north of the George Washington and Tappan Zee Bridges and out toward Tarrytown.

An elderly couple, Ellie and Max Kaplan, lived in the apartment across the hall from us and learned of our plight. They had raised their family in Port Washington on Long Island's North Shore and highly recommended we visit the town. The commute would be easy, they said, as trains between Port Washington and Manhattan's Penn Station made up at those destinations. We would not have to change trains anywhere. Once aboard, they said, you just hang up your coat and hat, read the daily newspaper, and in about thirty minutes you would be in the city. Max even gave me the keys to his car so I could drive to Port Washington and check it out.

I wasn't there ten minutes before I turned the car around and headed back to the city. *This wasn't the place for us,* I thought. *It was too small, just a little seaport town that probably didn't have a decent school system.* I could not imagine us living there. Before reaching the freeway I spied a real estate office, parked my car, and went inside. *Ellie and Max know us,* I said to myself. *They know what we like. If they believe Nancy and I would enjoy raising our family here, I've got to listen.*

As the realtor drove me through the area I realized I hadn't given Port Washington a fighting chance. There was a charm about the place I had not recognized. I was shown two homes Nancy might want to consider, as well as a lovely house on a quarter of an acre that had not yet been put on the market. The realtor arranged for us to see the house and it turned out to be just what Nancy was looking for, especially as it reminded her of her childhood home in Chatham, NJ. We purchased this Bayside Avenue home for all of $34,500. When we later moved to California, it sold for $56,000.

We had made an excellent choice in locations. It was worth the year and a half search. Port Washington turned out to be the ideal place to raise a family. Besides possessing a great school system there was a duck pond and a millpond, both great for ice skating when they froze over in winter months. For summer concerts there was a John Philip Sousa band shell overlooking a boat harbor. Jones Beach wasn't all that far away. The town boasted great eateries as well. Steak and lobster venues abounded. Sands Point was adjacent to Port Washington, a peninsula jutting out into Long Island Sound that had a working lighthouse with a red dome, right out of the story books.

Time passed, and the war in Vietnam had dragged on for thirteen years. In 1968 daily reports of the *Tet Offensive* filled the nation's television screens. There was no escaping it in the media; each network was competing with the other to see which could offer the most coverage.

One televised account that touched me deeply was witnessing the bodies of five young men from New Hampshire being brought back from Vietnam. As their flag-draped caskets were rolled onto the tarmac, a reporter described how their ton-and-a-half truck had hit a landmine on the way to the plane that was to bring them home. As I watched the airport ceremony unfold, recollections of the five Sullivan brothers going down with their ship in World War II flashed through my mind.

Turning away from the television screen I was drawn to the voices of my son Billy and four little boys playing with a toy helicopter in our back yard. In another minute the haunting sound of a bugler blowing *Taps* drew me back to the screen as an honor guard of Marines in full dress uniform stood at attention beside five flag-draped caskets.

Recalling images of my time in the Pacific, I sketched what I believed to be a likely sequence of events that lead to the demise of these young heroes. In the next days I put my thoughts to verse:

AND THEY WERE FIVE ©

They first touched down in a jungle spot, not
far from Company A, having gotten the nod to
join up with a squad who lost a few men that day.

It was late that night Charlie moved to strike
under cover of mud and rain. When the smoke had
cleared, though the five survived, replacements
were needed again, and again.

The faces of war were everywhere, like the scene
down the company street. There, with their
stares, through the barbed wire fence, hungry
Nams watched the GIs eat, and watched what was
thrown away. So much was thrown away.

Another face on a night patrol, a child hiding in
the grass. Frozen with fright in the raw night air,

chiggers and mites made a home in his hair. And
where was his mother? He had no mother.

Maybe the woman they found in a cave nearby would
take him in. They found her feeding a babe she
saved when the VC came for her kin. The boy?
She took him in. Why not? She took him in.

But now it's home for the five who served their
time in Company A. Young and strong and full of
life, it's back to the USA.

They loaded up in a ton and a half and drove in a
heavy rain, when a land mine exploded and ended
their lives before they could get to their plane.

And They Were Five, and the five came home.
Home, to the anxious hearts who waited,
Home, from the ugly war they hated.
Home to rest, to live no more.

(Here, the last three notes of Taps are heard.)

An NBC news editor felt I had captured the essence of the story and suggested I develop the verse into a short film. Further, he said I could find visuals to match the words by viewing Frank McGee's television documentary on the *Tet Offensive,* and that I could rent the footage from the NBC News Library.

After reviewing the archived tapes I selected and assembled relevant scenes and had them edited into proper sequence. After the film was assembled, Hugh McPhillips, an NBC producer, suggested I write a prologue and epilogue to the piece. Once completed I brought a camera and sound crew to my home in Port Washington and filmed the opening and closing sequences with five children from my neighborhood, including Billy. Coincidentally, he was five years old. When all segments of the film were edited to my satisfaction I wrote accompanying music and recorded the sound track at the Radio City Music Hall studio across the street from NBC.

And They Were Five begins innocently enough with five youngsters playing with a toy helicopter in a back yard. Suddenly we are transported into the harsh world of men at war. The five boys, now grown men, all die on the battlefield. They are brought back to their home town in flag-draped caskets one last time. In the final sequence of the film, the camera searches the empty yard as echoes of children's voices fill the air, a haunting evocation of innocence lost and lives brutally destroyed.

Films about war, many of which are controversial, have been popular throughout motion picture history. Some have glorified war: *Sergeant York, The Green Berets.* Many have attacked war: *All Quiet on the Western Front, Two Women.* Other films have been ambiguous: *Patton.*

And They Were Five delivers a powerful message that cries out against war, any war. While the eight and one-half minute film is no longer in circulation, in an exchange of correspondence with teachers over the years (mostly veterans of the Vietnam War), many have requested DVD copies which I have been pleased to make available to them. In return they have sent me stories, books and relative material on Vietnam which they used in their classrooms.

To view *And They Were Five* go to www.zabka.com

One treasured piece of literature in my collection is an autographed book with accompanying pictures, *Voices from the Ho Chi Minh Trail,* written and published by Vietnam veteran Larry Rottmann. In corresponding with Larry he told me he began teaching classes about Vietnam because his own children asked him questions about the war. He said he came to realize that the greatest therapy for him was talking about his experiences.

Author James Bradley captured what must be the universal feeling about war. In his book *Flags of Our Fathers,* he opens with a quote from a Japanese man, Yoshikani Taki, who said, *"Mothers should negotiate between nations. The mothers of the fighting countries would agree: Stop this killing now. Stop it now."*

THE DOCTORS

First Emmy in daytime drama, 1972
Norman Hall, Allen M. Potter, me, Hugh McPhillips

Ups and Downs

Concentrate all your thoughts upon the work at hand. The sun's rays do not burn until brought into focus.

—A. G. Bell

I was anxious for a new recording of *Christmas Eve in My Home Town* and was put in touch with Billy Sherrill, one of Nashville's more sought-after record producers. Besides recording Tammy Wynette, George Jones, Charlie Rich, Jim Campbell, Johnny Cash, and a host of others, Billy co-wrote many of their hit songs. I was on the phone with him for only a minute when he interrupted me by saying, "Yes, I know the song. It's good. I like it. As a matter of fact, I recorded it last night with Bobby Vinton. Do you want to hear it?"

I asked him how he knew of it, and Billy told me he was always looking for good songs and taped it off the *Tonight Show* when Kate Smith introduced it. "Do you want to hear it or don't you?" he asked.

"Yes," I replied. "Sure."

Afterwards, he asked me how I liked it. Risking my chance of obtaining a Sherrill-produced recording, I told him I thought the production was excellent but felt Vinton had veered off the melody in certain places.

"You are right," Billy said, "and I told him that. We are going to record the song again tomorrow afternoon, and if the (blankety blank) doesn't sing it like I tell him he can find himself a new producer." Sherrill then added, "And if the session turns out good, you will have yourself a hit record."

It was a good session and I did have a hit record. I still have Vinton's autographed copy of the sheet music dated August, 1970. As did Kate Smith, Bobby later sat down with me and taped individual Christmas greetings to our troops in Vietnam and around the world.

That same year Nancy gave birth to our second son, Guy Matthew. Billy and Judy were standing in the driveway of our house, waiting to greet him when he was brought home from the hospital. Billy placed one of Guy's tiny hands in his and shook it gently as if to say, "Hi, I'm your brother." Judy, impatient to hold him, raised her hands high and said, "See, Mom, they're clean."

I was finishing my fifth year on the daytime soap opera, *The Doctors.* We taped six one-half hour shows a week. Bob Myhrum, the principal director, directed four of the six, the first on Monday, the second on Tuesday, and two episodes on Wednesday. Hugh McPhillips, the associate producer, directed the fifth episode on Thursday. While assisting them with their shows I was preparing mine for Friday. We rehearsed and blocked all shows in the basement of the Edison Hotel off Times Square. After that we would trek across town to NBC to tape the show. On this particular day I was not prepared for what was to follow.

As we were leaving the Edison, Bob confided that he was stepping down as the show's principal director and asked if I would like to take his place. It was a flattering but tough question for me, as I didn't want to appear ungrateful. I had been offered a director's position on another show, but because of my music interests I respectfully declined. Directing is a huge commitment and a demanding one as well. If I intended to attain my musical goals I needed as few distractions as possible, however attractive they may be. My decision to decline Bob's offer was unalterable.

In the long run it was justified. Soon thereafter, a self-serving advertising agency representative was assigned to the show and proceeded to involve himself in producer functions. This did not sit well with our long-time executive producer, Allen Potter. As more and more of his authority was questioned or overruled he eventually resigned and moved on. *The Doctors* daytime serial was never the same. Minus his leadership its time slot on the NBC roster was frequently shifted in an attempt to regain top rating. Over the next several months many in the cast found it difficult to adjust to the radical change of tone on the set. A principal lead, Jerry Gordon, actually left the show altogether, deciding to seek his fortune in Hollywood.

I, too, eventually had a falling out with the agency rep when he chastised me for using my wedding song, *Take Thou My Heart,* in an episode which I directed. In a scathing memo that followed, the entire production staff was put on notice that only music cleared through his agency could be used without his permission. Wrong! Now he was assuming the province of music selection. There seemed to be no end to his meddling. When your work ceases to be fun it is time to move on, and that was the case with me. After five years I felt it to be in everyone's best interest if I turned in my badge.

It hurts when you feel you are well liked, when you believe your work is appreciated and yet you feel compelled to leave because of interpersonal tensions. For the second time in a few years my fate was to seek new vistas of opportunity. Perhaps these experiences were blessings in disguise. In any event, that is the situation in which I found myself. I valued my autonomy and integrity and felt at times I had to make tough decisions to keep both intact. Some of the changes were painful, but in the end I found most challenges to be interesting, if not stimulating.

Hurley's was a popular gathering place on the corner of 49th Street and Sixth Avenue. Documentary producer George Murray was there one evening, and over dinner we discussed the current television scene, how times were changing, and how creative talent was moving to the

West Coast. I asked George what project he was working on, and he told me he was preparing a television special based on countless tornadoes that had ravaged the Ohio River Valley that year. The one that he was centering on, he said, had devastated the historic village of *Xenia*. George was especially impressed with how its people had picked up their town by its bootstraps and pieced it together again. The title of his special was *Tornado, Xenia Ohio, 4:45PM.*

As George described his approach to the documentary project an idea came to me. I suggested that perhaps a running musical theme might be appropriate to connect the various aspects of his story, as in Edgar Lee Master's free-form poems, *Spoon River Anthology*. Regretfully, he said, he rarely used music in his documentaries because of budget restrictions. Seizing an opportunity, and on my own initiative, in the following days I composed a musical theme and played it for him. George especially liked the lyric, as he said the words reflected the emotions of the townspeople. Believing it might be a good vehicle for country singer Charlie Rich, I asked George for permission to present the song to Billy Sherrill, Rich's record producer in Nashville, and was given the go-ahead.

GONE ©

Where did a lifetime go,
Friends we used to know, not so long ago,
Where are they?
All are gone.
And where, the life we lived so free,
Days we laughed 'till night,
Nights we loved 'till day,
Where are they?
All are gone.

GONE,
All but the leaves of grass that fill the space,

GONE,
All but the mem'ries ling'ring round this place.

And yet, if life is still a friend,
Somehow all of us, standing side by side, will find a way

To live life now,
Not in the past,
But here, today,
Where we are now,
Where we are now.

Where did a lifetime go?

I waited eagerly for a response from Billy. If I were successful in obtaining a Charlie Rich recording, George said he would use it in his documentary. When the call came in, Billy told me he thought the music was a bit eighteenth centuryish for his taste but that he liked the song, and to "Come on down. We'll do it."

With great anticipation I boarded a plane to Nashville. Charlie Rich had studied music theory, had a good ear, and was a perfect match for the song. A Rich-Sherrill recording would be unbeatable. When I arrived at Billy's office I was told that Rich was nowhere to be found. He was out and about somewhere, that was all that was known. No one could find him. Larry Gatlin was offered the song but turned it down until he learned it was going to be the theme of an NBC special. He dropped into Sherrill's office to plead his case, but by then it was too late. Billy's producer friend Norro Wilson had brought in a young singer he was managing, and that is who recorded it.

I coached him on the song right up to the last minute, but he couldn't seem to get a handle on the melody. To his credit, it wasn't a simple song. Still, Billy recorded him anyway, and afterwards I played his rendition over the phone for George in New York. Rightly so, he said it fell short of what he was looking for. In order to give me something to take back to New York, Sherrill recorded the song himself. I didn't realize he had such a good singing voice. His was a fine recording, good enough to use on the show, but Billy said he was a producer, not a singer, and begged off. I couldn't talk him into it.

Confident that a running musical theme would contribute to Mr. Murray's television special, I could not let the opportunity pass. Instead, I invested in a recording session and hired Marty Gold to do an arrangement for orchestra and chorus. Glenn Campbell's brother Jim was available to sing the vocal lead, and he did a fine job. I conducted the session. Producer Murray came to the Radio City Music Hall studio, liked what he heard, approved the recording, and used it.

The gamble paid off. George's documentary pulled the highest rating in its time period at NBC and went on to win seven awards, including the Peabody and Christopher Awards for excellence in journalism.

"Gone" was my sixth major television theme, and brought me my third ASCAP Writer Award.

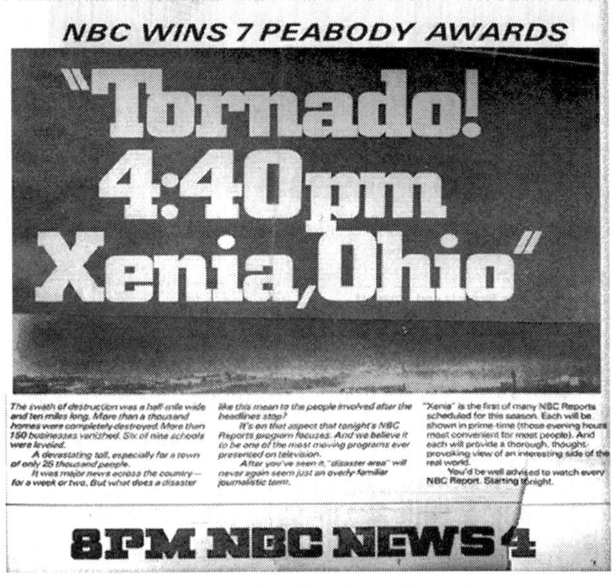

The music from this NBC Special brought me a third ASCAP writer award

I later submitted a recording of *Gone* to Frank Sinatra, but his manager sent me a polite letter of rejection. Actually, Mr. Sinatra probably never saw the music or listened to the song. Not too many people, writers or otherwise, crashed Frank's inner circle of professionals. On one occasion I did work with Sinatra and his arranger-conductor Nelson Riddle. It was in the nation's capital, when he produced a television spectacular in honor of newly elected President John Kennedy. I was associate director on the show. Every entertainer of note was on the bill, including the Mormon Tabernacle Choir. It was an ideal opportunity to get to know Sinatra better, but given my experience on *The Tonight Show* and *The Doctors,* I was leery about opening that door.

My theory was justified years later when I worked on *The Donny and Marie Show* in Hollywood. We were working on a Christmas program and because I did not ask the producer's permission to present my Christmas song to the Osmonds I was removed from the show. I was let go despite objections of the director who had hired me. Frankly, I could not fathom what all the fuss was about. Many creative people wear multiple hats. Carol Burnett's husband, Joe Hamilton, wrote the theme song for her show and no one fired him. But then again, he was Carol's producer.

I can only explain such unilateral actions with this analogy: In the early days of television creative talent was too often put in a box. If you were an actor or actress identified with a certain genre of the art, or if you were proficient in variety, news, sports, or whatever, you tended to be kept there. In my case, my area of expertise in television production was as an associate director and that was where I was encouraged to stay.

Still, I pitched my songs to outside sources whenever feasible. Arthur Godfrey was a big name at CBS in New York where he hosted his own variety show. Godfrey played a fairly good ukulele, and I penned a song for him, *Ukulele Polka.* I even brought it to him at a Boston hospital where he was recovering from some sort of illness. If he liked the song perhaps he would perform it on his television show. But

Godfrey was in one of his moods, refusing to see anyone, even refusing to accept the recording.

Orchestra leader and accordionist Lawrence Welk liked *Ukulele Polka* and wanted it for his television show, provided I re-name it *Accordion Polka* and change the words. For good or bad I chose not to do it, as I felt it was much easier to write a brand new song than to doctor up an old one. After Welk retired from the music business he left a publishing company worth millions of dollars. Mine could have been one in his vast catalog of songs. His letter to me is one of many in my scrapbook, along with letters of rejection from Barry Manilow, Andy Williams, Roger Williams, Bing Crosby, Frank Sinatra, and Dinah Shore.

I like to tell this story about recording star Perry Como: During one summer vacation Nancy and I were visiting her parents in Tequesta, Florida. "Mr. C." had a home on nearby Jupiter Inlet. I had worked on Perry's television show, had known his family, and decided to pay him a visit. I asked Nancy if she would like to join me, but she declined because I had not been invited. She said it was improper of me to impose. Technically she was right, but because I wanted to renew acquaintances with Perry I elected to visit him anyway. As I was about to leave, guess who was waiting for me in the car? Nancy said she didn't want me to get lost.

Perry's villa overlooking Jupiter Inlet was an imposing edifice, reminiscent of his home on Sands Point, Long Island. I was greeted at the door by a young nurse who was attending him.

Hearing our conversation, Mr. C. stuck his head around the corner and remarked, "Well, I'll be! Stan Zabka! What are you doing here? Hardly anyone visits me any more since Roselle passed away. Is your wife with you?"

Perry had huge hands, and when he shook yours it would become lost in his. He was a gracious, unpretentious man. A devout Catholic like Kate Smith, his Priest was always present back stage at the Ziegfield Theater where we televised his weekly variety show. During Nancy's and my brief but pleasant visit I danced around the question as to what his age might be. I explained that I myself never paid any attention to time or calendars or sundials, but as he always appeared so young, people would ask me how old I believed he might be.

"How old do you think I am, Stan?"

Attempting to be as discreet as possible, I ventured that he might be, maybe, sixty-five?

"Oh, no, Stan," he replied, "you are wonderful to say that. Actually, I am eighty-two."

In the official RCA Records *Billboard* magazine, *Mr. C's* life was summed up in these few words: "Fifty years of music and a life well lived, an example to all."

Of the hundreds of songs *Mr. C* recorded over the years, Perry claimed his favorite was one the RCA brass didn't want him to record. They said it would never sell. Perry never sang it in public, as he believed it would be disrespectful. The song was *Ave Maria,* probably his most successful and beautiful recording. It was my favorite too.

PART

III

The Making of a Mark

CHAPTER 18

The Giant Falls

I have only one command for you: be master.

—Napoleon

By the mid-nineteen forties NBC had established itself as the nation's undisputed leader in radio broadcasting. In 1946 its parent company, Radio Corporation of America (RCA), introduced something special. From its laboratory in Princeton, New Jersey, they unveiled an all-electronic color television system. The color was neither very good nor very true, but it was color. That same year NBC repeated what it had done in radio. With WNBC New York as its flagship station it proceeded to build the largest television network in the world. Sadly, in less than thirty years, the mighty empire would crumble.

Novelist Paddy Chayefski's Oscar-winning movie *Network* portrays a fictional broadcasting company's struggle for ratings by shifting the news division to its entertainment division. In his popular 1976 film the consequences of such action were severe, as his story centered on a news anchor who was killed because of bad ratings. Actor-reporter Peter Finch described the tenor of those times with his declaration, "I'm mad as hell and I'm not going to take this anymore." NBC's *Today Show* is an example of a program that was periodically shifted back and forth between its news and entertainment divisions in an effort to maximize the show's earnings potential.

After such a rapid rise to the top, what caused the fall of the NBC giant? I was an employee of the network from the beginning of those "Golden Years of Television" and was able to witness some of the contributing causes leading to its metamorphosis. NBC was, after all, the test tube baby for RCA inventions in radio and television. The network needed to bear its share of monetary obligations, and too often it fell short in that endeavor. Inside bickering with its show producers and stars, plus continuing differences between network brass and advertising agencies were contributing factors leading to its demise. One notable case that riled Johnny Carson was learning that NBC had destroyed the tapes of the early years of his *Tonight Show* programs, claiming they had no place to store them.

In its formative years, by successfully fielding these and other issues on a case-by-case basis the network enabled its music, variety, theatrical, news, sports and documentary divisions to move forward, separate divisions with a common goal. In the long run, the company was not able to survive the competition for resources, was constantly pitting one show against the other, refereeing talent squabbles, and dealing with ever-increasing external pressures for profit and market share. As economic and political pressures of the times took their toll it would be more than the structure could bear, and eventually it would collapse.

Location-wise, Rockefeller Center (NBC's home) is a business center, not a theater complex. A high rise office building is not the ideal location for dealing with long lines of people waiting to be ushered into audience participation or variety shows. Hence, traffic and security were issues to be dealt with. Theatrical presentations took their hit as well. Studio deliveries were usually made at night when street traffic was minimal around Rockefeller Center. These restrictive hours resulted in double and triple overtime pay for labor, an added deterrent not popular with producers struggling with ongoing budget restraints. Many of NBC's set designers were forced to downsize their scenery to fit into freight elevators not meant for that purpose, only to have to reconstruct their sets once they reached the studio floors. As ancillary and labor costs rose in one area they were passed on to other divisions, eventually affecting advertisers, sponsors, and ultimately the consumer.

Lacking ample studio space for its music, variety and game shows, NBC was forced to rent mid-town theaters—Ziegfield Theater, for example—for *Perry Como's Kraft Music Hall.* To accommodate rehearsals for its soap opera, *The Doctors,* the company secured the large basement room at the Edison Hotel in Times Square. For Max Liebman's *Your Show of Shows,* NBC rented the Park Theater in midtown Columbus Circle. To accommodate Bill Cullen's *Price is Right* game show and the *Steve Allen Tonight Show,* NBC rented midtown Broadway's Hudson Theater. For large presentations such as *Peter Pan* and *Hallmark Hall of Fame* the company built a huge sound stage in Brooklyn which added to commuting and shipping costs. In order to accommodate its ever-growing inventory of kinescopes and taped programs, the company built warehouses in New Jersey.

On a regular basis, NBC's music, variety, game show and dramatic presentations consumed huge pools of talent. The largest contingent came from Hollywood. Eventually, to save on travel, per diem and other production costs, many shows moved to the West Coast, including *The Johnny Carson Tonight Show.*

In the early 1970s, Broadway was having its headaches. Labor and management issues, coupled with theatrical, musical, and ongoing squabbles over jurisdiction forced the closing of many of its theaters. There appeared to be no reasonable end to these disputes. Sensing protracted periods of time without work many writers, producers, directors and artists packed their bags and followed their television counterparts (and some entire organizations) to Los Angeles.

By the early 1970s what was left at NBC? Its hefty schedule of dramatic shows that introduced us to Julie Harris, Richard Burton, George C. Scott, Richard Chamberlain, Helen Hayes, Paul Newman, Jimmy Dean—shows such as *Philco-Goodyear Playhouse, Masterpiece Theater, Robert Montgomery Presents, Matinee Theater*—were no more.

Music and variety shows that introduced us to Sid Caesar and Imogene Coca, *Your Hit Parade,* Milton Berle's *Texaco Star Theater*—creative productions that spawned such comedy giants as Howard Morris, Don Knotts, and Carl Reiner, were gone. As well, lucrative money-making game and quiz shows eventually came under attack. Many were forced to fold entirely as the Justice Department and assorted state agencies uncovered rigging and payola scandals. Today there may be no area of television more thoroughly policed than game and quiz shows.

By 1975 the only NBC shows remaining in New York were *NBC Nightly News, The Today Show, NBC Sports,* its award-winning documentary and specials divisions, and two soap operas, *The Doctors* and *Another World.* Meanwhile, behind the scenes, the company was cranking up a new variety show, *Saturday Night Live.* To accommodate that show the network completely rebuilt Studio 8H, the acoustics-perfect concert hall designed for the Arturo Toscanini symphonic broadcasts. In the final analysis, NBC shifted the bulk of its creative division from New York to Los Angeles, leaving its business and administrative divisions behind. Countless books on the "Golden Years of Television" are available, but from my vantage point that is what I witnessed.

With no regular show assignments a majority of the New York staff of associate directors, stage managers, and engineers bided their time reading magazines or playing cards in standby lounges, including me. We were protected by our unions, of course, but that was not the answer. In time our restlessness bordered on real concern for our futures. Approaching middle age I still had sufficient energy and desire to remain in the race, but found myself wondering what to do, which way to turn. I became irritable and developed an unhealthy attitude. Unrest and complacency impacted my home life. Something had to give.

In the past I had travelled to Hollywood twice a year with *The Tonight Show.* Many of my colleagues out west were now encouraging me to make a permanent move, to be where the action was. I had always wanted to write music for the movies and this seemed to be an opportunity to actualize this dream. Nancy sensed my growing concerns and urged me to investigate the potential. In March 1975 I flew out to Los Angeles. After meeting with music, television and movie people, I saw many opportunities for career advancement.

On my return to New York I met with my supervisor and requested a lateral transfer, but was refused. I considered the case closed until I learned the company had allowed two or three of its production and engineering staff to transfer to Hollywood. With that information in mind I hot-footed it across town to seek counsel from my union, the Radio and Television Directors Guild. I was offered no encouragement. I was told that if NBC asked me to transfer to one of its affiliated stations I could refuse, but the network was not obligated to grant a transfer based on a personal request. Well, there it was. I resigned myself to stay in New York.

Some weeks later a position opened up in Hollywood and it was offered to me. It was a stage manager job on *Days of Our Lives*. I had never worked as a stage manager. It is a demanding job. Besides controlling the stage itself, stage managers assign dressing rooms, coordinate makeup, wardrobe, and hair schedules. The logistics can be quite challenging, especially when working with temperamental talent and (sometimes not so talented) directors.

And then there are the ad agency people to deal with, some who assume the role of producer and wear their sense of responsibility like a shining halo, forever magnifying their sense of self-importance. Soap operas are big money makers for the networks. As I learned while working on *The Doctors,* producers carry a lot of weight. They are often on the set, and have a good deal of control over who goes and who stays, especially when dealing with casting and production concerns. A story is told of the famed movie director-actor, John Houston, whose friend had a cousin who had just graduated from film school. When asked how he might get started in the business, Houston's reply was, "Let him start at the bottom. Let him be a producer."

I was acquainted with the Hollywood stage manager I would be replacing; his name was Britt Lomond. When I asked my New York boss why Britt was leaving the show, he said it was because he wanted to work in film. As time was of the essence and a decision had to be made I was issued a take-it-or-leave-it ultimatum: "Zabka, the stage manager job opens in two weeks. You are familiar with soap operas. You worked on one for five years; you have a director's Emmy. Do you want the job or don't you?" Before I could reply, he added this prize little gem: "There is one hitch, Stan. If there is a layoff in Hollywood, you will be the first to be fired." Really? Well, that was nice. After twenty-four years with NBC starting out as a Page Boy, serving overseas with its Psychological Warfare Army Unit, winning a director's Emmy, writing and recording a half dozen of its show themes, I would be the first to be fired?

Nancy and I reviewed all the options and wrote them down. On the plus side I would have a job waiting for me in Los Angeles, a continuing health program for our family, and I would be in position to qualify for a home loan. The downside was that the burden of loading the wagon train and moving the family across country would fall on Nancy's shoulders. We weighed the pros and cons for some time and ultimately decided to make the move and get a fresh start on the west coast. We contacted a location company named Homerica to arrange for brokers to show us properties in the San Fernando Valley.

It was a tiring experience. We looked at a total of sixty-two homes in one week! At the end of a day we could not remember one house from the next. On the final day of our search we returned to the very first house we were shown and made the purchase. It was on Star Lane in Woodland Hills, complete with a swimming pool, basketball area and barbeque pit, and all the interior amenities Nancy desired.

The *Days of Our Lives (DOL)* studio in Burbank was just down the hall from *The Tonight Show* studio. NBC was undergoing studio modifications at the time and often many of the *DOL* dressing rooms were not available to our cast. Consequently, on many occasions it was necessary for me to assign available *Tonight Show* dressing rooms to some of the *DOL* talent. I would develop a queasy feeling in the pit of my stomach when I would meet up with some of my former *Tonight Show* colleagues. For years I had been the associate director on the show and here I was scrounging around for dressing room space. When I would see Johnny approaching I'd duck around a corner, not wanting to face him. I had left his show on a professional high as composer of his show theme, his associate director, his occasional guest and friend, and I simply didn't know what I would say to him if we bumped into each other. It was a pride thing. I hoped it didn't show.

Not always being assigned their regular dressing rooms definitely did not set well with one or two of the *DOL* super stars. Their feelings were made known to me on more than one occasion. Ultimately I was dismissed from the show over that issue, a decision that made absolutely no sense as I had no control over the dressing room situation. If I had not measured up to the professional standards of the previous stage manager it would have been understandable. Admittedly, I was not the best stage manager in the business, but I was not the worst either. Neither had I detected any sign of discord with anyone, cast or crew, that would have triggered a serious concern. The show had two directors and one associate director. Neither made mention of any problem.

After my dismissal from *Days of Our Lives* I was reduced to performing menial tasks timing commercials or shows. Eventually I was let go from NBC altogether, contrary to the agreement with my New York supervisor. There had been no layoffs. I was simply let go. Supposedly two NBC vice presidents intervened in my behalf, one who had been my roommate in New York when we were Page Boys. If either had actually made the attempt, their efforts fell on deaf ears.

In the past I had always been able to handle an unexpected turn of events and I felt I could deal with this one as well. I could have filed a grievance with my guild, but I was a new face in town and did not want to be considered a trouble maker. Perhaps it was the pride thing again. If it was, my reluctance to defend myself proved to be costly. Besides not having received any severance pay from NBC, I forfeited a good chunk of my pension. When I asked about the severance pay I was told that it should have been negotiated with NBC before I left New York. If at any time in my career I felt like cashing in my chips, this was it.

I was in for another rude awakening. Age had become an issue for employment. It did not take long for me to realize that in an industry dominated by a strong youth culture past credits on a resume, however strong, tended to unfavorably "date" a person. One vital truth became evident: anyone past the age of forty (like me) would be wise to get a skin tuck here or there, or submit to having tell-tale grey hairs darkened around the temples to at least appear younger. Married, with three youngsters of school age, a home mortgage on my hands and mounting bills to consider, I shook my head in wonderment at the mess I had fallen into. Attempting to sort it all out, I asked myself the proverbial question, "What are you doing in the middle of this field blowing this horn?"

You may remember Jack Paar, the urbane comic who preceded Johnny Carson as host of *The Tonight Show*. Critics rightfully credited this emotionally charged, unpredictable performer as having truly defined the talk show genre. Paul Keyes was Jack's head writer. When Paul left New York to seek his fortune in Los Angeles, Jack offered this advice: "Be careful, Paul," he said, "Here in New York they answer phones. They answer them in Hollywood too, if you are working."

I had been fired from NBC without cause, and no one felt obligated to tell me why. There was an ironic, almost sadist twist to the drama. A few months after I was let go a new associate director was hired, the son of the vice president who fired me. He had just graduated from television school.

I was literally out on the street. Any plans to write music for the movies was put on hold for an indefinite period. I was now a freelancer searching for work on my own, unfamiliar with knocking on doors and with handing out resumes. Prospects of obtaining a staff job at CBS or ABC networks were not all that promising, as the networks had full staffs of employees. A former New York friend, Bud Grant, now a vice president at CBS, introduced me to the *Carol Burnett Show* people and I was invited to sit in on many of their show rehearsals. On occasion I had lunch with Joe Hamilton, Carol's husband and producer. Unfortunately, there were no production openings on the show and apparently nothing looming on the horizon.

As I went around looking for work I came to learn that as an independent contractor, the requirements were more varied and more exacting as opposed to working in a specific role for a network. A special type of creativity and production savvy was demanded, more "thinking on your feet." No matter your job title, when you saw a hole you filled it, as you never know where your next paycheck might be coming from, and you needed to make a good impression at all times. The pace was faster too, because independent companies didn't throw money around like the networks. Word traveled fast in the industry. If you were good as an independent, you found work. If you were fired from a job, or otherwise let go, the reverse was true and it could take a year or more to recover.

Eventually I was able to land short-term projects. Harry Waterson, another of my New York friends now working in Hollywood, hired me for some shows he was managing for the Witt Thomas Company, among them a *Jonathan Winters* special. Bob Banner, who had been executive producer on the *Carol Burnett Show,* hired me to work on a Perry Como-Dick Van Dyke Mardi Gras special he was filming in New Orleans. Alan Landsburg, also from New York, hired me to assist him on a couple of television projects he was developing.

I received a huge break when Rudy Tellez hired me to direct a series of *Vidal and Beverly Sassoon* variety shows. Rudy was a former talent coordinator on the *Carson Tonight Show* in New York and was producing the Sassoon series. Accepting the directing job was risky for me. The show was non-union, a no-no for which I could have been fined by my guild, and so I directed under the name of Bill Stanley. Unfortunately I was not able to add the director credit to my resume; neither was my Sassoon Show salary able to be factored into my Directors Guild Health and Welfare Plan.

On Star Lane in Woodland Hills of the San Fernando Valley, money was going out of our house faster than it was coming in, and we were eating deeper into our savings. I needed to find a steady job, hopefully one that was long term. With mounting trepidation I decided to call in a marker. I had never sought return of a personal favor and it seemed demeaning to employ the tactic at this time. No matter! I picked up a phone and made the call. We switch to New York for the background.

When I was about to leave the *Tonight Show,* Dick Carson confided that he wasn't acquainted with NBC personnel and asked me if I would find a suitable assistant to take my place. I thought of one person in particular who would have been excellent, but he was not available at the time.

There was another fellow I thought to approach. Sager's Restaurant was just across the street from NBC, and one evening I went there for dinner after the show. Bobby Quinn was having a drink at the bar. He had once been associate director for Jack Paar, *The Tonight Show* host before Johnny assumed the reins. Apparently there was some sort of power struggle between Quinn and Kirk Alexander, Paar's director and friend. Paar got wind of it and fired Bobby who then found it difficult landing a new assignment. Instead, he was relegated to the mundane, non-creative work in Broadcast Operations Control (BOC) or working in Video Tape Central timing shows. Catching his eye at Sager's I asked him to join me at my table. After a brief conversation I explained that I was going to leave *The Tonight Show,* and that Dick asked me to find someone to take my place, and—was he interested? Needless to say, he jumped at the chance like a child with a new toy.

When the opportunity presented itself I put the two of them together and Dick agreed to give Quinn a trial run. He and Bobby didn't connect all that well at first. As a matter of fact there seemed to be a personality clash between the two. Each of them approached me separately with their concerns. My advice to both was to have patience, that over time I believed they would be good for each other. Eventually they hit it off and even palled around together to some extent. When Dick left the show to direct for Merv Griffin, Quinn took his place and remained director of *The Johnny Carson Tonight Show* until Johnny retired in 1992.

Finding myself in a similar position, I invited Bobby to join me for lunch at the Smoke House in Burbank, not too far from the NBC studios. Johnny had formed his own production company in Hollywood, Carson Productions, and I hoped there might be a job opening. I was too proud to contact Johnny directly and believed Bobby might pave the way. By now, as *Tonight* director, he was wired to the top, was close to Johnny, and was in a position to pull strings anywhere in town, but especially with my old boss. Bobby listened to my story and was, at least, a sympathetic listener. He indicated he would be glad to help, but cautioned me to be patient. "Johnny is going through a divorce," he said. "This is not a particularly good time for me to approach him." He asked me to give him a week or so, and he would get back to me.

That was the last time I saw or heard from Bobby Quinn. In the following twenty years I worked in Hollywood he never so much as bought me a cup of coffee. Friendships are important to me. Perhaps I counted too much on Quinn's returning a favor. Perhaps he never found the right time to approach Johnny. Or maybe, for whatever reason, Johnny said "no."

I would be extremely naïve to believe this sort of thing doesn't happen in any business, because I know it does. The question arises, am I bitter? The answer is, in the early days of my career I might have harbored some resentment, as it seems I was always struggling to maintain a balance, a level of stability between pursuing my music, my integrity as a man, and earning a steady income for my family. To this day I am convinced of one truth: *people aren't necessarily against you, they are just for themselves.*

Film director Robert Aldrich stated it more succinctly. In an interview several years ago he expressed his general attitude about playing the game in Hollywood:

> *Especially in this business, staying at the plate or staying at the table, staying in the game, is the essential. You can't allow yourself to get passed over or pushed aside. Very, very talented people got pushed aside and remained unused. That's the problem, staying at the table."*

THE LOVE BOAT CREW

Lauren Tewes, Gavin McLeod, Bernie Koppell,
Ted Lange, Fred Grandy

Crossover to Film

What you have inherited from your fathers, earn over again for yourselves or it will not be yours.

—Johann Wolfgang Von Goethe

In the early days the prevailing truth was that television was New York, and film was Los Angeles. You worked in either one or the other, rarely in both. In fact, television and film professionals were represented by two separate guilds, The *Radio and Television Directors Guild (RTDG)* and the *Directors Guild of America (DGA)*. That disparity changed in 1960 when the two guilds merged into a more formidable union, the DGA.

Generally, movies are made by a single film camera establishing a scene and then moving it from position to position for cover shots or close ups. Television employs multiple video cameras. When I came to Los Angeles in 1975 it wasn't uncommon to walk onto a Hollywood movie lot and see film crews wearing tee-shirts with the imprint "Tape Sucks." Maybe so, but as the medium was growing by leaps and bounds the writing was on the wall: check it out. Among the first film pioneers to switch to multiple camera use was comedian-director, Jerry Lewis.

Visiting a movie lot or television stage was always a big thrill for my kids. Judy wrote in her journal: "We would get to do things with dad that no other kids could, see the different shows, like *Love Boat*. I thought it was so cool that I got to meet all those neat actors and actresses and that my dad was a director, go brag about him at school and things like that."

Love Boat! I remember that television series well. Our first episode was in May of 1977. We filmed a show a week at the 20th Century Fox Studios. The set was so spread out and some of our scripts so busy that we hired at least a dozen extras a day. When the script called for a swimming pool scene an additional dozen were needed. That was great, because as the show's second assistant director my job was to cast the extras, and I enjoyed hiring people.

One of the directors who came aboard to do an episode of *Love Boat* was the husband of the realtor who sold us our house when we moved to L.A. His name was Jack Arnold, a film director from the old school especially noted for his innovative science fiction movies. Jack did not find the crossover to multi-cameras all that satisfying, and as many in our principal cast had never worked in film they weren't comfortable with his directing style.

Late one afternoon as he was leaving the studio Jack approached me at my trailer where I was signing out some extras. Apparently feeling he could confide in me, he asked if I knew what he was doing wrong on the set. Since he asked my opinion I explained what I had observed. He was doing nothing wrong, I said, he just needed to adjust his pace from single to multiple cameras, put aside the fact that he was a famous film director, and gear his attitude more towards the needs of his players.

Following *Love Boat*, I moved up to first assistant director status on *Greatest American Hero* featuring William Katt and Robert Culp, and was able to get Billy a minor acting roll in one of the episodes. After shooting a scene at our local *El Camino High School* we filmed an additional sequence in our house a few blocks away. That was the last time I allowed my home to be used as a shooting location, as the crew was not all that considerate of our furniture or rugs. To top it off, when it came time to filming a scene with Culp, I often found him in my den making long distance phone calls on my private line.

After *Love Boat* I went over to Universal Studios to work on *The Eddie Capra Mysteries*, a television series about a lawyer named Eddie Capra who helped solve some of L.A.'s most baffling crimes. One of my alternating first assistant directors was Larry Powell, who joined the series mid-season. Larry was a World War II P51 fighter ace and a retired Army Air Force colonel who was in high demand on films like *Tora Tora* and *Midway* where all types of aircraft were involved. I wanted to be a fighter pilot myself, and could hardly wait for the opportunity to work with Larry on his movies.

Until I could cross over into films I had been working off and on in television for four years. About that time my wife Nancy entered the real estate business and met up with a former college friend, Gail Sickinger. Gail was married to Neil Maffeo, Vice President of Lorimar Pictures, and the company that produced *The Waltons* television series. During dinner at their home Neil asked if I had considered working in film. I replied that I had, except that the Directors Guild said I needed an additional year of California residency and then pass a series of film entry tests. Neil said he believed he could resolve the guild issues, especially given my long history in television production. Three weeks later the film offer came in, a second assistant director's job on a Movie of The Week, *Streets of L.A.*, starring Joanne Woodward.

My first days on *Streets* were a disaster. On one particular shooting day we were filming at a shopping center, and I committed a huge blunder by sending two dozen extras to the wrong location. Had it not been for our transportation captain discovering my error, they might still be on the street corner waiting for the shooting company. Fortunately, I was able to return the whole bunch to the proper location in time for camera setup.

I was happy Neil had given me a job, but I don't think he did my first assistant director (1AD) any favor. All heads of departments report to the 1AD who essentially runs the company: camera, lighting, grips, transportation, catering, makeup and wardrobe, special effects, the works. A Second AD (2AD) reports to the 1AD and does the grunt work. On *Streets of L.A.*, my 1AD was a girl. This was her initial assignment in that capacity, and here she was saddled with an assistant who had never worked on a movie and didn't even know how to fill out a cast and crew call sheet.

In the end we managed to finish *Streets* on time and on budget, everyone was happy, and my 1AD survived the ordeal and went on to new assignments. Actually, we worked together on another picture, the name of which escapes me at this time. It was another Movie of The Week. I later was privileged to work with other fine actresses besides Joanne Woodward, talented ladies like Helen Hunt and Shirley MacLaine. On *Streets,* Joanne especially liked sushi for lunch, and that is mainly what I ordered for her. Sometimes her husband, Paul Newman, would visit the set. All he wanted was a cold beer.

Setting a shot for Perry Como's New Orleans TV special

My good friend, Production Manager Larry Powell on the movies set of Bronco Billy

When Larry Powell moved into live action films he took me along with him. In the process I came to know another flying great, Art Scholl. The movie industry lost its best stunt pilot when Art's bi-plane crashed mysteriously into the ocean off San Diego while filming Paramount's *Top Gun*. His last words to the crew were, "I've got a problem here." Only pieces of the wreckage were found. Art's most notable stunt was the "lomcevak," the Czechoslovakian word for "headache". The stunt involves a series of forward and end-over-end somersaults. It was banned in East European countries because of its danger. I watched Art performing the maneuver in *Red Flag*, a movie on how the Russians trained their pilots for combat missions.

General Chuck Yaeger was brought on board *Red Flag* as our technical coordinator. Chuck was the first test pilot to fly his plane faster than the speed of sound. Today his Bell XS-1 aircraft hangs in the National Space and Air Museum alongside the Wright Brothers *Flyer* and Lindberg's *Spirit of St. Louis*. We shot the main body of film at Nellis Air Force Base in California with a *Blue Angel* flight squadron and F-16C Aggressor aircraft. Once that portion of the movie was completed the company travelled to Las Vegas for some added scenes.

On weekends the cast and crew were free to do chores, make phone calls or visit the casinos on the strip. I needed to do my laundry, and was loading a bag of it into my car when General Yaeger pulled up alongside me in his truck. "Are you heading for the Laundromat?" he asked. "I just came from there. Throw your stuff in back and I'll take you there. Don't worry about soap or quarters, I have plenty." To pass the time at the Laundromat we walked around the block and chatted. Actually, I just listened as this living legend assisting me with my laundry revealed anecdotes from his amazing career. When *Red Flag* wrapped, Larry presented me with a lithograph of Chuck's plane, *Glamorous Glennis*, numbered and autographed by the general. It hangs on the wall in my den, a prized possession.

Following *Red Flag*, I worked as second assistant on *The Rebels* in a cast that included Don Johnson and Doug McClure. Andrew Stevens starred as Philip Kent, an English nobleman who traveled to America to fight alongside the colonists in the Revolutionary War. John Jakes, noted author of the trilogy *The Rebels, The Bastards, The Seekers,* was a DePauw University graduate like myself. He visited *The Rebels* set on occasion. I would like to have introduced myself, but never found the opportunity. Had I known that we had attended the same school I would have made it a point to greet this noted author.

General George Washington sought winter quarters for his men in Valley Forge, Pennsylvania. We filmed that portion of *The Rebels* in the snowfields of Northern California. It took a full week to complete what was scheduled as a three-day shoot. Equipment and truck engines froze. Tents were lifted from their moorings as strong winds whipped through the area. Horses and pack animals had to be sheltered from the icy weather until they were brought onto the set. Portable heaters were set up near the cameras and the film canisters loaded just prior to shooting a scene. We hired one hundred extras from the surrounding areas to serve as Continental soldiers. These townspeople were accustomed to freezing weather, but this storm proved to be too much for many of them. As had happened in Washington's army, many deserted. On any given day it was not unusual to see one or two rag tail recruits out on the road, thumbing a ride back into town.

From the beginning on *The Rebels,* communication between the director and the first assistant was not going smoothly. As the voice of the director, the 1AD has to deliver what the director needs. It is a very tight collaboration. During the Valley Forge sequence my 1AD told me he planned to quit, and I strongly advised him against it. This was his first assignment in running a large film company, an opportunity to prove he could deliver the goods under adverse conditions. I advised him to try to work through his difficulties with the director, which he did, and to his credit he went on to establish a fine career in the industry.

When Clint Eastwood hired Larry to be production manager on the film *Bronco Billy,* I was brought along as second assistant direc-

BRONCO BILLY IN NEW YORK

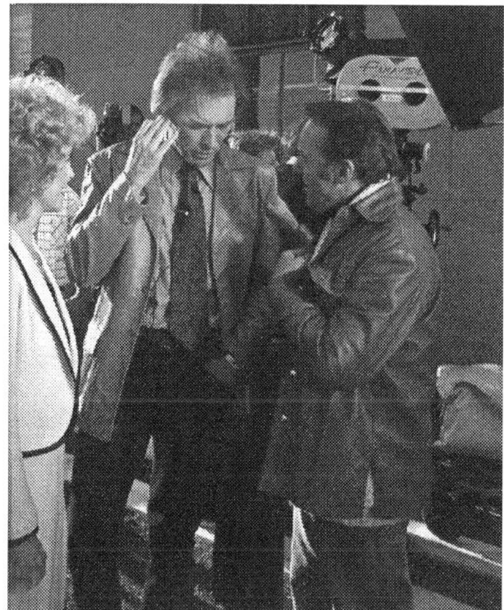

Me with Director/Star, Clint Eastwood

tor. The main portion of the movie was filmed in Boise, Idaho. Clint directed and starred in it. In my opinion, having come to know him to a certain degree I felt his portrayal of *Bronco Billy* to be the personification of the true Clint Eastwood.

Sandra Locke was his co-star in a cast that also included Geoffrey Lewis and Scatman Crothers. It was my first film for Clint's Malpaso Productions where I was privileged to meet and know Bob Daley, Clint's former partner and executive producer. Up to this point I probably learned more about film making from Eastwood than I had from any other director. Clint is not known for doing multiple takes of any particular scene. If he likes what he shoots, he prints it and moves on to the next setup. One time at the camera when things got bogged down he said, "gentlemen let's not think this to death, let's shoot it."

One particular camera setup troubled me, and I decided to question him about it. There was a scene in the movie that called for *Bronco Billy* (Clint) and his five circus friends to rob a passenger train. We were in the middle of nowhere. Billy chased the train on horseback while his five circus partners raced after it in an open, red convertible. Once that scene was filmed, the camera was set up for cover (close-up) shots. The train had been filmed going in one direction, and a cover shot was being filmed from another angle. How it would cut in editing puzzled me. Since I had never worked with Clint I was not sure he would be open to questions. Thankfully, he was. I don't recall his exact words, only that he told me I had caught something no one else had, but he felt the angle would work in editing and was going to keep it.

Principal photography was completed in Boise, Idaho, ahead of schedule and under budget, additional factors for which Eastwood is known. This is almost a contradiction, as he is said to over-budget knowing he can bring the film in at a lesser cost. There was a closing scene in *Bronco Billy* that needed to be filmed in New York. Clint wanted to shoot the scene in a certain apartment, but a Manhattan location company was unable to obtain permission. Knowing the city as I did, Larry felt I might be able to secure the site and presented the idea to Clint and Producer, Bob Daley. The next thing I knew, I found myself on the way to my old stomping grounds instead of returning to Los Angeles with the rest of the crew.

The apartment Clint wanted was featured in an *Architectural Digest* magazine. It was located in the Black Tower, a prestigious high-rise luxury complex on Fifth Avenue, directly across the street from St. Patrick's Cathedral. Jackie Onassis maintained a suite of apartments there as did many other notables, including royalty. Residents of this swanky dwelling were not all that impressed with show people, and weren't excited about anyone invading their privacy.

Malpaso is a first class production company. Larry put me up at the Plaza Hotel off Central Park. My first line of business after settling in was to phone my friend Jerry Plano and enlist his help in getting me into the Black Tower. That very evening Jerry invited me to an RCA Records Division party where I was introduced to an executive who actually owned one of the apartments in the complex. Through him I was able to secure the apartment Clint wanted. I lucked out. Considering how hostile the Black Tower management was toward film companies, I was happy the effort paid off.

Having secured the permit and completed my assignment, I checked out of the Plaza and joined my wife and family who were vacationing in Florida. I had hardly unpacked my bags when I received a call from Larry saying that Clint wanted a balcony on the apartment, one that had a clear line of sight down Fifth Avenue to the Statue of Liberty. That was nice, I replied, except there were no balconies in the Black Tower. Further, I explained, I didn't believe there was a building in all of Manhattan with a clear line of sight to the Statue of Liberty. Larry's comment was, "Stan, Clint wants a balcony."

The next morning I was on a plane back to New York. A day later I hooked up with Producer Bob Daley, who flew in from Los Angeles on the Warner Brothers jet. As soon as he could unpack his bags and catch his breath we set out from the Plaza to investigate every logical rooftop and balcony in Manhattan. We even investigated those that did not have a line of sight down Fifth Avenue as Clint had hoped for. Believing the Waldorf Astoria might hold the answer, we checked it out. However, it presented multiple, insurmountable problems like air conditioners and chimneys obstructing views in every direction. Next, we decided to visit the Black Tower management to see if we might obtain permission to build a balcony on its rooftop. We could open the scene there, cut camera, and then move inside the apartment for interiors. Just as I had suspected, for security and other reasons, our request was denied. We could have the apartment, but that was all.

One possibility remained, and that was Rockefeller Center with its half-a-dozen tall buildings. Bob and I toured the complex with its superintendant and found our location, on the rooftop of the Eastern Airlines Building. It was just what we were looking for, offering a spectacular view of Manhattan as well. A nighttime scene from this perspective would look great on film. Problem solved, Bob headed back to Los Angeles on the Warner jet and I stayed behind to attend to the logistics of building a balcony on the Eastern Airlines building.

That completed, I was just about to check out of the Plaza and return to Los Angeles when I received a phone call from Larry instructing me to remain in New York and complete the filming. "And by the way," he added, "you have been upgraded to Production Manager-Second Unit Director." That was a nice surprise! Before hanging up, Larry added, "One other thing: Tom Snyder at NBC wants to do a television interview with Clint. If you can fit it into the schedule, set it up."

And so I stayed in Manhattan to finish the film. To be honest, I enjoyed returning to New York with the King of Hollywood and being able to arrange an interview for the network that fired me just years before. "What goes around, comes around," as the saying goes.

The biggest challenge I had in setting up the Snyder interview was being able to find ample time to get Clint into an NBC studio. The only way I could see it happening was to have Snyder and his crew join our company on the Eastern Airlines rooftop and conduct the interview after we completed filming our balcony scene. Running the idea past Clint, that piece of business was locked in.

Once again Larry was on the phone from Los Angeles to say the film editor needed a transition shot indicating that Bronco Billy's lady friend (Sandra Locke) had left the circus to return to her home in Manhattan. The scene was this: actor William Prince's limo would round a corner, pull over to a news stand, pick up a newspaper, read the headlines "Heiress Returns to New York," and drive away. Clint wanted to film this pickup shot on Park Avenue, mid-town. That was well and good, but the problem was Park Avenue did not have newsstands, and even if it did, there was no time to obtain a city permit. In addition, providing a permit could be obtained, when could we film the piece? No need to ask the question; I knew what Larry would say, "Stan, Clint needs the news stand scene."

As I pondered how and when to do it, I remembered a funny character I had seen on television that would go around Manhattan digging up holes. He would select a busy sector like Times Square, have his crew set up a canvas protection screen in the middle of the street, and then start drilling away. No one questioned him. He had no permits, of course. He merely wanted to prove he could get away with doing anything he wanted to in the big city. He was a riot. I forget his name.

To film the news stand scene I found a location that would work for us, the corner of 57th Street and Park Avenue, and a very busy intersection. The only way I could see us filming the shot without a permit was to do what this television character did, steal it. I explained to Clint that after filming the rooftop scene, and while he was busy doing the Tom Snyder interview, I would take a cameraman and William Prince and shoot the Park Avenue segment. I would have everything prepared and rehearsed the day before. A news stand loaded with magazines and newspapers would be set in place at the last minute. As William Prince's limo pulled around the corner, my camera operator would appear out of a store doorway, grab the newspaper scene, and we would be out of there. And that's what we did, without a permit. If we had been caught, we would have been fined. But we would have the film!

Before returning to Los Angeles I received one more phone call, but this one was not from Larry. It was from Tom Snyder, inviting me to dinner. He wanted to thank me for having arranged the interview with Clint. I politely declined his kind invitation, as I considered returning to NBC with Clint Eastwood was reward enough. Nancy once said that sometimes it is okay to give ourselves permission to brag about an accomplishment, and I must say that in this instance I felt pretty good. It was a classic case of rejection turning into reward.

Any Which Way You Can, (the "monkey" picture), was another movie I worked on with Clint. We filmed it in Sun City, North Hollywood, and Bakersfield, California, ending the film with a major fight sequence staged in picturesque Jackson Hole, Wyoming. There was a scene in the movie where a horny motel manager had eyes for elderly Ruth Gordon, one of his motel guests. Whenever this old codger would see Ruth he would visualize her prancing out of the water in the young, curvaceous body of Bo Derek from the movie, *10.* The script called for a second film unit to shoot the beach scene with a Bo Derek look-alike.

ON LOCATION

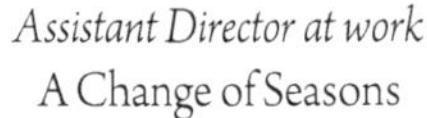

Assistant Director at work
A Change of Seasons

... starring Miss "10," Bo Derek

Ruth Gordon's face would then be edited into her body. However, rather than doing the scene in this manner, I had another idea and ran it by management. Instead of filming the beach scene with a Bo Derek double, why not use the original *10* footage with the real Bo Derek exiting the water?

Earlier, when I was with NBC I had worked with a little-known special effects system known as Rotoscoping whereby one feature in a frame could be removed and another inserted in its place. In this case, we would be inserting Ruth Gordon's face on Bo Derek's body. This would be a bit tricky to accomplish technically, because in the movie *10,* Bo is not walking, she is jogging out of the water. I checked with technical experts at Warner Brothers and they assured me the plan would work.

First, however, we would need permission to use the footage from Bo Derek's movie, "*10.*" Clint was confident we could obtain the clip as Blake Edwards, the film's director, was a friend of his, with the same agent. Clint instructed me to make the call and to let him know if there were any problems. In the final analysis, the Rotoscope experiment was not successful, as the Ruth Gordon face insert did not appear natural. It looked pasted in, so management reverted to plan A, filming the beach scene with a Bo Derek look-alike.

Earlier I had an opportunity to work with Bo on *A Change of Seasons* in New Hampshire, a movie which co-starred Anthony Hopkins and Shirley MacLaine. My brother Bob's son, Britton Zabka, holds patents as creator of holograms. I was wearing one of his creations that reflected the image of a cross, and Shirley asked if she could wear it for awhile. That was some time ago. I wonder if she still has it.

Bo's husband, John Derek, was Bo's constant companion and an excellent photographer. Before Seasons wrapped he gave me a copy of an *Esquire* magazine which contained photos he took of Bo au natural. During the filming of *Seasons,* John took dozens of location stills. Rarely would he be seen without his trusty camera. I got to know the Dereks well. They were a fun couple to work with.

When *Seasons* wrapped I returned to Los Angeles and received a phone call from the head of production at MGM in Hollywood. He said the Dereks were going to make a *Tarzan* movie in Sri Lanka and wanted to know if I would consider coming aboard as production manager. Bo would star in the movie and John would direct. This was a flattering offer. On *A Change of Seasons* I was only second assistant director.

In a production meeting at MGM, John explained the variables under which he wanted to make the film, conditions which I found to be risky, if impractical. There would be no shooting schedule per se. Instead, Derek wanted to work free-form, charting daily activity as he saw fit and making changes as he went along. To film in this unorthodox manner, at a distant location, on the budget I was shown, required some investigation. While I was grateful for the opportunity to work on the film I explained that I had just finished my third consecutive movie, and before I signed on to the *Tarzan* project I was hoping to visit with my family. In the meantime, I promised to read the script and review the budget, and to be available for questions.

The MGM executive felt my request to start in two weeks was reasonable. After a period of silence, Bo spoke up. "What do you think, John? Stan says he will do it."

"I don't think so," John replied. "He wants to be with his family."

That ended the discussion and the chance to work with Bo and John Derek. In retrospect, learning of some of the Sri Lanka problems encountered in the filming of *Tarzan*, I questioned whether I would have had the temperament required for the assignment.

I enjoyed being with the family again. The kids seemed to be growing like weeds. There was always something going on, and time seemed to fly by. It must be true that an apple doesn't fall far from the tree. Having visited television and film sets over the years our children, Billy, Judy, and Guy, eventually found their way into the business. Many of their friends were doing milk and other commercials and our kids wanted to get into the act as well. From the outset, however, I made it clear that there would be no complaints if they were not chosen for a part, especially since Nancy and I would be their shuttle bus to auditions.

Being on a film set was more than a passing fancy for Billy. He was forever putting on a costume or mask and filming skits in the neighborhood with his trusty eight millimeter camera. When I booked him as an extra on *Love Boat* for a full week he caught the acting bug big time. In 1984 his commercials agent sent Billy on a series of auditions to play the role of Johnny Lawrence in a movie, *Karate Kid*. Billy had just come home from the gym. "I don't know what they are looking for, Dad," he said. "I have read for them

Billy Zabka *Ralph Macchio*

three times already." My answer was to go back and just be the part, not to act it, but to be tough, and that is what he did.

Apparently Billy duly impressed the director, John Avildsen. The problem, he told Billy, was that he was bigger than Ralph Macchio who had already been cast in the lead.

"Didn't you receive an Oscar for directing 'Rocky'?" Billy asked, "because Sylvester Stallone was smaller than the person he fought."

Billy had presented a convincing argument. "Yes, he was," John replied. "And you've got the part. Who is your agent?"

After the success of *Karate Kid*, Reverend Robert Schuller invited Billy to be guest speaker at the *Crystal Cathedral* church to talk about the movie and to share his testimony. In part, Billy said, "When you become the role, or the role becomes you, you relate to it. There is something about the role that is inside of you and you pull that forth, and that is what Johnny was in me. Johnny was a part of me that most people do not see."

Besides watching John Avildsen at work on the *Karate Kid* set, another film director I admired was John Chapman who began as a cameraman on Steven Spielberg's movie, *Jaws*. Later John distinguished himself by moving up as director of photography on the Martin Scorsese epics, *Taxi Driver* and *Raging Bull*. Chapman then made his own directing debut in the movie *Clan of the Cave Bear*, followed by *The Annihilator*, a sci-fi film about aliens planning to conquer the earth. The plot centered on halting an invading android army. The script was loaded with special effects. I was Chapman's first assistant on *The Annihilator* and was quick to recognize how adept he was in creating complex camera movements and improvising on the set.

Ours was a busy shooting company, changing setups and making major moves on the spot which often involved timely adjustments of cast, crew and equipment. We filmed chase scenes, blew up everything imaginable, and burned a building or two at one of our distant locations at California's Lake Arrowhead. It was an exciting experience for me, and I was grateful for the opportunity to work with Chapman and the crew.

When we wrapped *Annihilator* to return to Los Angeles, John motioned me to sit in the front seat of the limo, saying I deserved it. He said I was a big factor in bringing the film in on schedule and on budget with no one getting hurt in the process. I mention this not to boast, but to make the point that directors of Chapman's caliber attain such heights because they are uniquely confident people, comfortable in their own skin. For someone to be so gracious as to acknowledge the assistance of others in reaching his goals is an attribute I learned, admired and appreciate to this day.

I had come to Los Angeles to write music for the movies, but that opportunity still had not presented itself. I had some mouths to feed and needed to seek steady employment, or something akin to it. With a director's Emmy for *The Doctors* to my credit I decided to seek work in that capacity and signed on for representation with the Irving Salkow Talent Agency. Finding work at this level is a tough nut to crack in Los Angeles unless you are well known. Irving was not successful in finding me work as a director, but he did introduce me to David Wolper who hired me as first assistant on *Collision Course,* a Henry Fonda special he was producing on the General MacArthur-President Truman controversy during the Korean War.

Following *Collision Course* I worked as a first assistant to Robert Zemeckis on his film, *Romancing the Stone* and later with Robert DeNiro on *Midnight Run.* Larry Powell was production manager and hired me to run the Second (Stunt) Unit of *Midnight Run.* We crashed twenty-five police cars daily, or at least a good number of them. The main cast and crew of the movie were housed in Sedona, Arizona. A Navajo Indian reservation outside Flagstaff was staging area for our vehicles and three aircraft.

On one major shooting day we staged a helicopter, fixed-wing aircraft, and a two-dozen police car chase through the town and hills of Sedona. Seven cameras were placed along the one-mile route. Six production assistants with walkie-talkies blocked traffic at crucial intersections as we readied the scene. One local Sedona resident wasn't all that happy being detained. This fellow had gone into town to do some shopping and wanted to get home. When I explained the stunt to him, that he would be able to see a major Hollywood ground-to-air chase being filmed, he could care less. "I left Hollywood to get away from you SOBs," he said. A jug of Jack Daniels from a local grocery store calmed him down long enough for us to film the action and move on.

Nancy (and other wives of the crew) was able to join us in Arizona, something not always possible to arrange when a movie company is forever changing locations. Ushering in the New Year in picturesque Sedona was a wonderful experience. Two years prior, while working in Hong Kong with Chuck Norris, and still later with the *Dallas* company, I wanted to bring Nancy to the orient to show her that exciting part of the world, but busy film schedules didn't permit.

In 2003 Nancy and I traveled to Europe to watch the filming of *MOST,* written and produced by our son Billy, and directed by Bobby Garabedian. *MOST,* in Czech language, means "the bridge," and tells the story of a father who tends a draw bridge under which boats pass and over which trains are allowed to cross. The drama that unfolds at the bridge when the father's young son goes to work with him one day is the key element in this true story. The main body of the movie was filmed in Prague, the Czech Republic, while the bridge sequence was filmed in Szczecin, Poland.

While Nancy and I enjoyed watching our son make his first movie we were not content just to sit around idly and twiddle our thumbs. Consequently, Nancy volunteered to help out as set photographer and I assisted in filming the bridge and train sequences. After the film was completed, our songwriter son Guy later added his creative talent by contributing some music to composer John Debney's inspiring score.

Movie buffs will find the revealing "behind-the-scenes" story on the making of *MOST* a primer on the trials and tribulations (and satisfaction) of independent filmmaking. The bridge in Poland is the only

OSCAR LUNCHEON 2004

Stacie & Billy Zabka *Bobby & Elkin Garabedian*

remaining draw bridge of its kind left standing in Europe after World War II, and remains operational. The train which was used in *MOST* was the one used in filming the classic movie, *Piano*.

The making of this Oscar-nominated film *MOST* was epic movie making, dealing with a draw bridge that gets stuck while filming in the icy cold of winter, of fighting with Royal Sun Alliance to honor a bonding agreement, of returning a year later to successfully complete the film when the weather did not match. In the end, to have escaped Prague with the film intact during the worst flood in a hundred years, adds to an almost incomprehensible drama.

Before returning from Europe, Billy, Nancy, and some of the crew and I motored from Prague to the small Czech village of Bystrice (pronounced Bis-tree-chee) where my father was born. It was a rewarding experience visiting the little church where he was baptized and to tour the castle that guarded the picturesque town where he grew up.

This side trip turned out to be a very special addendum to an already eventful trip to the Czech Republic. Here was a country invaded and ruled over more times than probably any other in Europe. To witness its free people in so dramatic a Central-European setting, the land of my parents, was most gratifying.

Every five years since the end of World War II the town of Pilsen conducts the *Celebration of the City of Pilsen.* May 6th, 2010, marked the 65th anniversary of the liberation of Pilsen by General George Patton's Third Army. This is how the people of the Czech Republic remind the world how much they love America and the American Soldier.

Had we not traveled to Europe to make a movie, we may never have visited so lovely a land or come to know such grateful, hard-working, friendly people.

ON THE AIR...
OVER THERE

"The Soldier's Christmas Song"

CHAPTER 20

The Soldier's Christmas Song

There is a space between man's imagination and man's attainment that may only be traversed by his longing.

—Kahlil Gibran

I believe music is the principal link that unites people in both mind and spirit. Dozens of songs have helped keep hope alive and home fires burning, especially in times of war. In writing this book I created a chapter on the history of songs that brought us through World War II. Some of the memorable songs of that era were *Praise The Lord and Pass The Ammunition, Sentimental Journey, I'll Walk Alone, I'll Be Home For Christmas, We'll Meet Again, Don't Sit Under The Apple Tree (With Anyone Else But Me), GI Jive.*

I researched the authors of these and many more musical gems, the recording artists or the bands that made them famous, and who controlled the copyrights. Unfortunately, I had to put the work aside as the long and arduous task of tracking down publishers, writers, estates or owner-controller of the works proved to be an endless ordeal.

It was in tracing the history of these songs that I realized our country had been involved in eight military conflicts since World War II, beginning with the Cold War with Russia. In 1950, Korea ushered in war number two. In 1955 Vietnam became number three, and Grenada in 1983 was number four. But it was number five, the Gulf War and Iraq's invasion of Kuwait that brought our government face to face with an issue not heretofore connected to the battlefield, but yet was vital to the morale of our troops.

It was at that time, just months before Christmas of 1990, when hundreds of songs written by and recorded for loved ones serving in the Persian Gulf flooded headquarters of the Armed Forces Radio and Television Service (AFRTS) in Los Angeles. As government clearing house for music, news, sports, and other programming, AFRTS approval of all broadcast material is mandatory. That was the case when AFRTS wanted to make Christmas music available to our troops serving in the Persian Gulf. There was major problem. Our government forbade it. Kuwait was a Muslim country.

One month after our troops entered Kuwait, September, 1990, I received a phone call from Master Sergeant C. Brandon Williams, AFRTS Broadcast Chief. The sergeant asked if I would come to his office and speak with him about our government's restriction on Christmas music, saying he might have a solution to the problem. His plan was to create a series of broadcasts labeled *Desert Shield Mailbag,* and he wanted permission to use my Kate Smith–Johnny Carson interview on *Christmas Eve in My Home Town* to kick off the series. Kate had appeared on the Tonight Show with Johnny in 1966 after she had recorded the song and taped Christmas greetings to our troops in Vietnam. That was twenty-four years earlier, a long time ago! To think that Sergeant Williams believed the program might still be relevant was hard to imagine. His comment was, "After all, who was to tell our troops they could not receive mail from home, even if it was in the form of a song?"

His hunch paid off. Using the Kate Smith-Johnny Carson interview to spearhead his request, the government waived all restrictions and gave Sergeant Williams permission to proceed. Just in time for Christmas, his *Desert Shield Mailbag* programs were taped in Los Angeles and broadcast via satellite to AFN headquarters in Frankfurt, Germany, then relayed to Dharan, Saudi Arabia. From there the signal was forwarded to the Navy Broadcasting Service and finally to Army Mobile Detachments One, Two, Three and Six in the desert.

On Pearl Harbor Day, December 7, 1990, an unexpected letter from the US Department of Defense thanked me for helping facilitate the AFRTS *Desert Shield* initiative and "for bringing the musical message of Christmas to troops who otherwise may never have received it."

Two years later, March of 1992, America became involved in war number six, Bosnia-Herzegovina. As in the Persian Gulf, our government had no mobile units in those locales. Once again, *Desert Shield Mailbag* programs were beamed by satellite to our troops in that area in time for Christmas. Via such initiatives our Department of Defense has ensured our service men and women overseas that information and entertainment from home was made available.

Nine years later, September of 2001, the infamous date referred to as "9/11," al-Qaeda Islamist terrorists based out of Afghanistan destroyed the World Trade Center in New York City and part of the Pentagon in Washington, DC. War number seven had begun. Two years later, March of 2003, the invasion of Iraq ushered in war number eight.

Two members of my extended family who had served in both Bosnia-Herzegovina and Afghanistan were deployed to Iraq. One was my brother Bob's granddaughter Brooke, a Captain and Black Hawk helicopter pilot. Brooke's former husband, Captain Roger Maynulet, was a tank commander serving in the same area. Learning of my involvement with AFN, Roger wrote to me from Iraq explaining the desire of troops in his command for news, sports and music from home. His letter went on to say the only broadcasts they were receiving were three hours of satellite feeds from the Voice of America and some news from England ("the Brits,") as he called them. Everything else, he wrote, "is in Arab."

What was needed, he said, was an AFN broadcasting station in Baghdad itself, saying it would be of great value not only to his troops, but to the locals in his command:

> *The Brits broadcast news and some music via satellite on a different station 24-7, but I don't know if they have the enhanced sensitivities we do for other cultures. I don't think people understand that our culture (rock 'n roll, MTV, Hollywood, etc.) is our best weapon to turn the youth in this country to be pro-American. The religious clerics fight it hard because they know it's their biggest threat and it's much harder to bomb MTV and Tom Cruise than one of our patrols.*

In another of his letters, dated the 26th of November 2003, he went on to say:

> *Depriving our soldiers of this morale booster effectively ties one hand behind our back by not showing the benefits of western democracy (and all it brings, liberated and educated women, and the fact that there is life out there beyond the mosque.) It's frustrating, but at least we have AFN on our Satellite TV, all eight channels. They have been airing promos about the AFN-Europe sixtieth anniversary, and showing some of the founding fathers. I'm waiting to see you there.*

The AFN anniversary celebration Roger referred to had taken place in Baltimore, MD, just two months previous, the twelfth of September, 2003. At that time I was privileged to meet guest speaker, General Robert E. Gaylord, Chief, Army Public Affairs. In conversations to follow, I asked for his assistance in bringing *Christmas Eve in My Home Town* and other yuletide songs to Iraq. I was surprised to learn from the general that he had been commander of the Desert Shield/Desert Storm broadcast network during the Gulf War. As such, he told me he had personal knowledge and appreciation of the history of the song and its contribution to our military members serving overseas. General

Gaylord assured me he would look into the music matter on his return to Washington.

Of further concern, however, was the need for our government to establish an actual AFN broadcasting unit in Iraq. In discussing that issue with General Gaylord I presented him with copies of the correspondence I had received from Captain Maynulet. I was not prepared for the speedy action that followed.

Three months later, just in time for the Yuletide season, a full-blown, working AFN broadcasting unit went on the air in Baghdad, with permission to air previously forbidden Christmas music. In the mail I received the following article from General Gaylord:

Stars and Stripes, European Edition
Monday, December 8, 2003
AFN-IRAQ HITS BAGHDAD LATER THIS WEEK

American Forces Network-Iraq will begin live radio broadcasts from Baghdad this week, featuring news, weather, music, tips on Iraq's culture and language, and other content tailored to troops in the country. The station is operated by the 222nd Broadcast Operations Detachment, a US Army Reserve unit out of California.

General Gaylord declined to accept credit for this, saying the action had been accomplished through the combined efforts of Colonel David R. Apt, Army Broadcast Service, along with "a lot of hard-working young folks." His letter to me said:

Dave and his staff will coordinate directly with AFRTS in regards to airing Christmas Eve in My Home Town to our service members serving in Iraq over the holidays. In addition, your material will be provided to Mr. Kane Farabaugh, the AFN Producer for our AFN 60th Anniversary documentary, which will air in six segments throughout the year. Your detailed

> *and colorful story of Christmas Eve in My Home Town and its unique lasting relationship with AFRTS military broadcasting will find its way into a broadcast tribute to AFN Europe.*
>
> *Respectfully,*
> *Robert E. Gaylord*
> *Brigadier General*
> *US Army Chief of Public Affairs*

Four years later, in 2007, Nancy and I travelled to Reno, Nevada, to attend what may prove to be AFN's last reunion. Former AFN broadcaster Nick Clooney, Distinguished Journalist in Residence at The Newseum in Washington, DC, accompanied by his lovely wife, Tina, was guest speaker for the event. An old buddy, Andy Guthrie, former AFNer and broadcaster with the Voice of America was there, arrayed in his Scottish kilt. Gary Bautell, Director, AFN Europe, flew in from Frankfurt, Germany for the reunion. During the weekend festivities Gary outlined his vision for a special broadcast on the story of *Christmas Eve in My Home Town* and its longtime connection to our troops. Gary asked me to send him as much information on the song and its history as possible, plus recordings by Eddie Fisher, Kate Smith, Bobby Vinton and Jim Nabors.

In a return letter to me dated the ninth of August 2007, Gary said:

> *Your package arrived a couple of days ago. It's fantastic. It's great material. I've already talked to Lieutenant Colonel Malcolm and he is as enthusiastic about the project as I am. The radio special might end up as a TV project as well.*

Three months later, on Pearl Harbor Day, Friday, December 7, 2007, a special package containing AFN radio and television programs on *The Soldier's Christmas Song* were delivered to my door. Written and narrated by Gary Bautell and AFN broadcaster, Michelle Michael, the programs were broadcast to some 300,000 service members and their families in Europe, the Middle East, Iraq, and Afghanistan. Gary also

DIRECTOR, AFN EUROPE

Gary Bautell

informed me that both specials were made available by satellite to AFN networks in Korea, Japan, and DTS (Direct to Ship) to the Navy.

Here at home the AFN story of Don Upton's and my Christmas song appeared in *Playback*, the quarterly magazine of *the American Society of Composers, Authors, and Publishers* (ASCAP).

To view Michelle Michael's AFN telecast go to www.zabka.com

As for the American Forces Network, it remains a unique force in broadcasting annals. Having worked with all of our stateside networks, I can say unequivocally there is none other quite like it. It is as much alive today as when General Eisenhower gave AFN its start in England in 1943, and Major Glenn Miller's Orchestra initiated the first AFN broadcast with its swing arrangement of *American Patrol.*

I feel both honored and fortunate to be part of the AFN broadcast tradition and credit the network for providing the world-wide audience and notoriety *Christmas Eve in My Home Town* may never have enjoyed. How many songwriters are afforded such a wonderful opportunity?

One of the most beautiful choral renditions of the song was arranged by Mark Hale conducting the magnificent 135-member *Masters of Harmony* Choral Group. You can find it on YouTube or elsewhere on the Internet.

MY FAVORITE FAMILY OUTING PICTURE

Guy, Judy, Nancy, me, and Billy

CHAPTER 21

Giving It Back

When I stand before God at the end of my life, I would hope that I would not have a single bit of talent left, and could say, "I used everything you gave me."

—Erma Louise Bombeck

Grass Valley is the place Nancy and I have called home since we moved here from Los Angeles in 1995. We found a cozy townhouse that seemed like a great place to hang our hats for awhile, unpack some things, and become familiar with the surroundings. Little did we realize it would remain our residence for almost twenty years, although returning to a warmer climate when cold weather sets in is often a topic of discussion. Grass Valley is located in the foothills of the Sierra Mountains where gold was first discovered. We enjoy the change of seasons, the coming of spring and the kaleidoscope of color in the fall. In the winter, when snow blankets the ground, the North Country is a veritable wonderland of white. On a clear day you can get a glimpse of Lake Tahoe's snow-capped mountains.

We are fortunate that our daughter Judy and her family live nearby, although we miss seeing Billy and Guy and their families in Los Angeles and Nashville. Still we try to manage frequent visits and otherwise stay in touch through texting and telephones. As a group, however, I can't recall a Thanksgiving or Christmas holiday when we weren't all able to get together.

Having lived and worked in a music metropolis like New York I still find the aesthetic environment in Grass Valley to be somewhat similar. I'm not referring to the "industry" excitement or buzz, but to the genuine love for music and the arts expressed here in so many creative ways. Various *Music in the Mountains* concerts and *Blue Grass* festivals are popular, drawing devotees to our Nevada County Fairground from all over the country. Travelers arrive in their RVs, campers, and vans and park under the trees for days at a time engaging in song fests around campfires. Dueling banjos, the strum of guitars, and sometimes the sweet sound of a solitary violin can be heard long into the night after the park has been closed for the day.

Theater draws many devotees here as well, along with various arts and crafts displayed during seasonal festivals. The nearby wine countries of Sonoma and Napa Valley with their excellent restaurants and cuisine stage a variety of festivals. After reading his biography, *Harvest of Joy*, Nancy and I were pleased to be introduced to the late wine impresario Robert Mondavi and his charming wife and artist, Margrit.

On many an occasion we visited filmmaker Francis Ford Coppola's winery in Napa. I don't know if it is still there today, but upstairs of the spacious wine-tasting room was a museum with his show business artifacts, Oscars, theatrical awards, and his father Carmine's music scores. Displayed in an adjacent room were all sorts of memorabilia, including a Tucker automobile from one of his movies. Coppola is to the world of movie-making as Mondavi is to wine-making. Both Italian, driven men, their approach to life and work differ only in tempo and style.

When I lived in New York I watched Francis direct one of his early movies, *Rain People*. At that time I had no idea I was observing a film icon in the making. When my son Billy's film *MOST* was making the rounds of the film festivals I took him and my son Guy to visit the Coppola Museum. Viewing Francis's Oscars and awards, Billy said he'd be satisfied if his own film would just win an Oscar nomination, a wish that became a reality.

Although I miss some of the big city atmosphere I'm happy San Francisco is just a few hours' drive from our place. Next to New York City, the "city by the bay" is my favorite. Both are alike in many ways except that New Yorkers tend to brag about their city while San Franciscans are content to allow visitors to discover its greatness for themselves. Musically, however, they have one thing in common: both San Francisco and New York have had wonderful songs written about them, and equally great recording artists to sing their praises.

New York is referred to as the place people like to visit but wouldn't want to live. Of late I have had ample time to reflect on three factors that make up that city: Manhattan's *stability* is said to come from the foreigners who first settled there, from the families who were born and raised there, and from the outsiders who came to visit and decided to stay. Its boundless *energy* is derived from the multitudes that travel to and from the island via its network of tunnels, subways and bridges. The *romance* of New York is the product of the steady stream of travelers who arrive from all parts of the world to tour its museums, attend its theaters, visit Times Square, and to pay homage to the revered "lady with the lamp."

I have heard it said that a person can visit a place, but can never go back, especially if he's been away for a spell, and I think that is true. As varied as my fond memories are of New York, and as special as the feelings I retain for the city, I do not believe I could ever live there again. On second thought, that statement may be somewhat of a contradiction. Having been raised in Chicago, served in the Pacific, attended college in Indiana, soldiered throughout Europe, and worked a half century in towns and cities around the world, the plain truth is I really grew up in Manhattan. The city gave me life when I needed it, a home to grow my talents, and a place to find myself when it was necessary to stretch my abilities, test my desires, and fulfill any need or pleasure in an atmosphere of wonder and excitement. It was New York that provided the foundation and substance that would forever shape my career in the arts, the most fulfilling profession I can imagine. And it was in New York that I met the lady who would become my soul mate and life partner.

When we first moved to Grass Valley Nancy and I enjoyed precious moments with two of our little grandchildren, Michael and Katie. One afternoon while they were down by the creek throwing rocks, Michael made a remarkable discovery. As one pebble after another disturbed the water's surface, its ringlets fanning out into a chorus of larger and still larger circles until they disappeared, he asked this question: "Where did all the circles go, Grandpa?"

Good question, Michael, I thought. *I often ask that about time.*

At my advanced age I have actually gained a new lease on life by entertaining at retirement and assisted living homes. Performing before captive audiences I seem to have come full circle and am back on the stage once again.

I average at least six engagements a month. Sometimes there are only a handful of people in the room, sometimes it's packed. I do a sort of Victor Borge routine at the piano. Since most people at these facilities are seniors we share a like sense of humor. As such, I intersperse my music with light-hearted jokes to help break the ice: "I can always tell when I am getting older because when I bend down to tie my shoes I ask myself, 'What else can I do while I'm down here'?"

I always get a laugh when I tell the joke about a senior citizen who calls to his wife to come upstairs for some romance, to which she replies, "Honey, I can't do both." I also like the one about an elder couple sitting on the veranda sipping wine. The lady says, "You know, I don't think I could go through life without you." The man responds with the question, "Was that you talking or the wine?" "It's me talking," is her response, "and I'm talking to the wine."

What better audience than these to share events of my days in show business? The look on their faces when people learn that I have worked with Johnny Carson and others is almost priceless. I certainly do not consider myself a celebrity, but in these moments I am made to feel like one. I am the closest many of these folks have ever been to a major artist, and so their interest level heightens exponentially. It's quite revealing, actually.

Being cooped up in their rooms a good part of the day, the "wrinklees," as my brother Bob calls us, want to hear mostly happy songs. I try to encourage everyone to sing along with me. *You Are My Sunshine* is probably their favorite. It is amazing to witness the spirits of these people come alive. At the beginning of the hour some of their heads may be completely sunken into their chests, as if they are asleep. But by the end, if I'm successful, I may notice a few fingers drumming a beat or see some toes tapping. Inevitably, a few smiles can be detected.

Bottom line, more than having provided some entertainment, I leave these facilities satisfied that I have added something special to their day in a manner that I find in no other activity. Physically, senior citizens are most likely experiencing common bodily aches and pains.

I feel that explaining how I cope with mine encourages many to give my "home remedies" a try.

I explain how I exercise my arthritic fingers by opening and closing them repeatedly during morning walks. Otherwise, I explain, I would hardly be able to play *Chop Sticks.* I tell them how, in driving my car to their facility, I do voice exercises to open my vocal chords. I tell them how I pray for an hour of energy that my head and hands cooperate so I can get through the hour. Sometimes I get emotionally distracted by the audience and forget the key I am playing in, the words to the songs, or the chord progressions. In the long run I figure if I make a mistake, and everyone is having fun, chances are they won't notice my mistakes anyway. Or if they do notice, they won't care.

When I entertain, some ask my age. To evade the question my response usually is, "What's today?" A silly reply, but it provokes a laugh. Few people care to admit their age until they reach their later years, and then they tend to brag about it. When I thought I was turning thirty-nine, my wife said, "You are going to be forty, babe. Add it up."

Invariably, after a performance many guests want to chat. All seem to have a story to tell. Some, I've discovered, have been singers or musicians themselves, or writers, or knew people who were. One particular resident said he was vocalist with the great Frankie Carle Orchestra. I'm a big fan of the Frankie Carle piano style and perform a medley of his hits, including *Sunrise Serenade, Moonlight Cocktail,* and *Autumn Nocturne.*

It seems modern technology has not only altered how we conduct business but how we communicate with each other as individuals. We do not write letters or use the telephone as we used to. I have never been much of a techie or multimedia person, but in order to keep pace with family and friends I try my best to stay as current as possible.

Many senior citizens are not interested in the Internet. They say it is too demanding, takes too much time, or that it requires too much patience. Perhaps another reason is they prefer to hide within their own shells, not realizing the personal gifts they have to offer.

For me, smart phones, social networking, and the ever-changing world of communications have charged my batteries and stimulated my creative juices. Were it not for computers replacing typewriters I doubt if I would have completed this book. Now I find others are tackling their memoirs as well. Whether they finish or not doesn't matter; the important thing is they have begun.

If there is one lesson I have learned that I can pass along to a younger generation of aspiring entertainers, should that be their goal, it is one spoken to me by my musical son, Guy:

> *The ideas we have, the television shows, the songs or movies we create are extensions of who we are. But all are merely seeds of promise yearning to bear fruit, and will remain dormant unless cultivated.*

Guy makes a good point. I have always been amazed at how weeds survive while habitually being trampled on and crushed, while supposedly strong flowers wilt and drop from the vine. For myself, when the winds of opposition tempt me to pack my bag of longings too soon, I have an expression: "Nulle bastardo carborundum!" (Don't let the bastards get you down!)

In my two-year journey writing this memoir, Nancy has been a major force in tracking significant events as to the what, when, where, and how of what happened in my life journey. Recently I discovered an envelope she put on my desk with an attached note that said, "Since you are writing your story you might find a place for this somewhere." It was the *Notes in Passing* letter I had written to her when I finally came to terms as to the true nature of the world of entertainment and my place in it. The letter was written a year after we were married:

October 16, 1965
To my dear wife, Nancy,

Do not make me out as someone more than I am. I am someone struggling to find his way in a business where guts, more than talent, win out. And I find myself spending more time developing my guts than I do my talent. But for that I can fault no one, the industry, the people connected with it, the problems inherent in it. Nor can I blame the public who indulge our inventions. For we all, each of us, are a product of our time, and while we are swept up in the onrush of time and its dictates we find ourselves either compromising ourselves to the turn of the moment or standing, sometimes seemingly alone, attempting to lead. In that attempt, good or bad or mediocre as we see it as individuals, is where time is lost, wasted.

We should be perfecting where we are instead of fighting. And who knows in the end if our effort has been good, or bad, or mediocre. For in the end we have little time to evaluate. And that is so because we go on to our next task, to fight the fight instead of learning and developing our God-given gifts. But in the end, isn't the struggle also the theme? Don't we also learn by being in the race?

It has been said, if I recall the quotation, that "The race is not always to the swift." I seek no race, only the pursuit of my talents if, indeed, I have any in the long pull of things. And so I try.

And I stumble. There is a market for my works. It is in the marketplace that I labor the longest hours. It is that which I would like to change. I wish I knew how much my worth is, musically. Maybe only time will tell.

Thank you, friends, for hanging with me until
The End

ABOUT THE AUTHOR

Stan Zabka

The zest and talent of Uncle Stan is impossible to present in one short paragraph. He is a talented musician who chose the difficult road of the entertainment field. He is a composer of music, some of which made the hit charts: *Christmas Eve in My Home Town, Chimes, Take Thou My Heart,* and *Searching Wind.* For those of you who are interested, he has a CD, *Zabka's Themes From Television.* Beyond his musical talent, Uncle Stan worked as associate director of the *Tonight Show* with Johnny Carson and produced/directed several Hollywood motion pictures and productions. He graduated from DePauw University and served in WWII and the Korean War . He and his loving wife Nancy live in Grass Valley, California. Their creative talent shine through three grown children: William (Billy), Judy and Guy. This is certainly a family of fun, and Uncle Stan brings much of it to the table. His silly antics, love of a good laugh and generally good-natured disposition make him a joy to be with. Beyond the fun he is a man of perseverance and great gumption. He will climb any mountain if there is a new experience to be had and a reward that will afford him a new and creative opportunity to live again.

—Jami Irene Boarman
Stan's niece and daughter of Dr. Clifford Zabka

Connect with Stan and his music at www.bigislandmusicinc.com